WAL★MART®

Family Cookbook

Don's Deep-Dish Pizza
page 27

Good food and great recipes are meant to be shared. That's why each year we invite Wal-Mart associates to submit their favorite recipes — particularly those that their friends and families ask for over and over again — for publication in our Wal-Mart Family Cookbooks. In this 2007 edition, we proudly present what we consider to be some of the best recipes in the country.

So get cooking! Have a few friends over for dinner. Treat a loved one to a special meal. Create a wonderful weekend brunch for ...nd most of all, g and sharing ipes for many

D1294891

Try-Foods International, Inc.
333 Semoran Commerce Place
Apopka, Florida 32703

Special thanks to:
All of the Wal-Mart Associates who entered
their recipes in the contest.

WAL★MART®

- Garnishes may have been added to enhance photographic images.
- Use caution when handling hot peppers. Wear disposable gloves or wash hands thoroughly after preparation.
- Keep your hands and all surfaces and utensils that come into contact with food clean.
- Separate cooked or ready-to-eat foods from raw meat, poultry, eggs, fish, and shellfish.
- Follow the doneness tests accompanying each recipe to assure reaching a temperature that destroys harmful bacteria.
- Keep hot foods hot and cold foods cold.
- Thaw frozen foods in the refrigerator—never at room temperature.
- When in doubt about the safety of a food, throw it out.

At the time of publication, all Associates were
employed by Wal-Mart Stores Inc.

The Wal-Mart Associate recipes featuring Bertolli pasta sauces
were not provided by Unilever.

Printed in USA
First Printing, 2006

desserts

brand recipes

Artichoke Dip

ingredients

2 cans (13.75 oz. each) artichoke hearts,
   drained and cut up
1 cup **Kraft® Shredded Swiss Cheese**
1 cup **Kraft® Shredded Parmesan Cheese**
1 cup **Kraft® Shredded Low Moisture
   Part-Skim Mozzarella Cheese**
1 cup mayonnaise
Bagel chips

directions

1 Preheat oven to 350°F. In large bowl combine artichokes, cheeses, and mayonnaise. Place in shallow 2-quart baking dish.

2 Bake for 15 to 20 minutes or until heated through. Do not overbake. Serve with bagel chips.

MAKES 20 (1/4-CUP) SERVINGS.

Nancy Borth
Wal-Mart *1479   Valparaiso, IN
This recipe, shared by another associate from Nancy's Wal-Mart store, has since been enjoyed at family gatherings and is a requested recipe.

Chili Cheese Snacks

ingredients

2 pkg. (3 oz. each) **Philadelphia® Cream Cheese**, softened
1 cup **Kraft® Shredded Cheddar Cheese**
1/4 cup canned chopped green chile peppers
1/4 cup chopped ripe olives, drained
2 tsp. **McCormick® Minced Onions**
1/4 tsp. bottled hot pepper sauce
2 pkg. (8 oz. each) refrigerated crescent rolls

directions

1 Preheat oven to 400°F. In small bowl beat cream cheese with electric mixer for 30 seconds or until smooth. Stir in Cheddar cheese, chile peppers, olives, onions, and hot pepper sauce.

2 Separate each package of crescent roll dough into 4 rectangles, pressing perforations to seal. Spread about 3 tablespoons of the cheese mixture over each rectangle of dough. Starting from the long side, roll up. Cut each roll into 10 slices.

3 Place slices, cut sides up, on baking sheet. Bake for 9 to 12 minutes or until golden.

MAKES 80 APPETIZERS.

Judith L. Cope
Wal-Mart #1319   Knoxville, TN
These tasty snack bites are excellent to serve at football parties or other casual get-togethers, according to Judith.

Chinese Egg Rolls

Marty Bullmer
Wal-Mart *143   Hickory, KY
Marty says that this is a family favorite recipe that she and her husband developed together.

ingredients

1 1/2 lb. ground pork or chicken
6 tbsp. soy sauce
1 medium head Napa cabbage, shredded
1 carrot, shredded
1/2 cup fresh or canned bean sprouts, rinsed and drained
1 can (8 oz.) water chestnuts, chopped
28 egg roll wrappers
1 egg, lightly beaten
Enova™ Oil for deep frying

directions

1 For filling, in large skillet cook pork until brown. Stir in 2 tablespoons soy sauce. Transfer to large bowl; set aside. In same skillet cook cabbage and 2 tablespoons soy sauce until cabbage is just wilted; transfer to bowl with pork. In same skillet cook carrot, bean sprouts, and water chestnuts in remaining soy sauce for 3 to 5 minutes or until carrot is tender; stir into pork mixture. Strain mixture; discard liquid.

2 For each egg roll, spoon about 1/4 cup filling just below center of wrapper. Fold bottom corner over filling, tucking under on other side. Fold side corners over filling. Roll egg roll toward remaining corner. Moisten top corner with water; press firmly to seal. Brush egg roll with egg.

3 In a large saucepan or deep-fryer heat about 2 inches of oil over medium heat to 365°F. Carefully add egg rolls, a few at a time; cook for 2 to 3 minutes or until golden brown. Serve warm.

MAKES 28.

Crab Rangoon

ingredients

1 pkg. (8 oz.) **Philadelphia® Cream Cheese**, softened
8 oz. imitation crabmeat chunks, finely chopped
2 to 3 green onions, finely chopped
1 tbsp. **McCormick® Minced Garlic**
1/8 to 1/4 tsp. **McCormick® Cayenne Pepper**
50 won ton wrappers
1 egg white, beaten
Enova™ Oil for deep frying

directions

1 For filling, in medium bowl stir together cream cheese, imitation crabmeat, green onions, garlic, and cayenne pepper. Cover and refrigerate for 30 minutes.

2 For each, place 1 rounded teaspoon cheese mixture in center of won ton wrapper. Brush edges lightly with egg white. Fold squares in half, bringing opposite corners together to form triangles. Press edges to seal.

3 In large saucepan or deep-fryer heat oil to 375°F. Carefully add won tons, a few at a time, to hot oil and cook for 30 to 60 seconds on each side or until golden. Remove with slotted spoon; drain on paper towels. Serve warm.

MAKES 50.

Connie Kroneman
Wal-Mart *2335   Dane, WI
Connie says that these appetizers are best if served warm but also are tasty when cold.

Cranberry-Orange Spread

ingredients

1 pkg. (8 oz.) **Philadelphia® Cream Cheese**, softened

2 tbsp. frozen orange juice concentrate, thawed

1 tbsp. sugar or **SPLENDA® No Calorie Sweetener, Granular**

1/8 tsp. **McCormick® Ground Cinnamon**

1/4 cup chopped pecans

1/4 cup dried cranberries

4 tsp. finely shredded orange peel

Buttery crackers

directions

1 In medium mixing bowl beat cream cheese, orange juice concentrate, sweetener, and cinnamon with electric mixer until combined. Stir in pecans, cranberries, and orange peel.

2 Cover and refrigerate at least 1 hour. Serve with crackers.

MAKES 12 (2-TABLESPOON) SERVINGS.

Mary Botosh

Wal-Mart #1672   Iron River, WI

When she brought this spread to a company potluck, Mary says everyone loved it so much that she shared her recipe with everyone.

Grandpa Dean's Onion Dip

ingredients

1 medium onion, chopped
1 tbsp. **Enova™ Oil**
2 pkg. (8 oz. each) **Philadelphia® Cream Cheese**, softened
2 tbsp. Worcestershire sauce
1/2 to 1 tsp. salt
1/2 to 1 tsp. **McCormick® Ground Black Pepper**
1 to 2 tbsp. milk
Assorted crackers or chips

directions

1 In small saucepan cook onion in oil until tender.

2 In small mixing bowl beat onion mixture, cream cheese, Worcestershire sauce, salt, and pepper with electric mixer on medium speed until fluffy. Gradually beat in enough milk to make of desired consistency. Cover and refrigerate at least 2 hours before serving. Serve with crackers.

MAKES 20 (2-TABLESPOON) SERVINGS.

Alida Fischer
Wal-Mart #1632 Alexandria, MN
Alida's father has had this recipe since the early 1950s. The creamy dip has shown up at many family gatherings, social events, and football games.

Ham Ball

ingredients

2 cans (5 oz. each) chopped fully cooked ham, drained and flaked
1 pkg. (8 oz.) **Philadelphia® Cream Cheese**, softened
1/4 cup mayonnaise
1/2 tsp. yellow mustard
1/4 tsp. bottled hot pepper sauce
1 tsp. **McCormick® Minced Onions**
1 tbsp. **McCormick® Parsley Flakes**
1/2 box (15 to 16 oz.) buttery crackers

directions

1 In medium bowl combine ham, cream cheese, mayonnaise, mustard, hot pepper sauce, onions, and parsley flakes.

2 Place mixture on plastic wrap. Wrap tightly while shaping into a ball. Refrigerate 8 hours or overnight.

3 Just before serving, finely crush 8 to 10 crackers. Unwrap ham ball and roll in crumbs to coat. Serve with remaining crackers.

MAKES 20 (2-TABLESPOON) SERVINGS.

Norma Moore
Wal-Mart #1319 Knoxville, TN
For a relaxing night of television or spending time on the patio, Norma enjoys this simple, savory appetizer spread.

Mexican Dip

ingredients

1 can (16 oz.) **BUSH'S® BEST Refried Beans**
1 carton (16 oz.) sour cream
1 pkg. (1.25 oz.) **McCormick® Original Taco Seasoning**
2 cups **Kraft® Mexican Style Shredded Cheese**
1 jar (16 oz.) salsa
1 medium tomato, seeded and chopped
1/2 cup chopped green onions
1 jar (8 oz.) taco sauce
Tortilla chips
Veggie chips (opitional)

directions

1 Preheat oven to 375°F. Spread refried beans in bottom of 3-quart rectangular baking dish. In small bowl combine sour cream and taco seasoning. Spread over refried beans. Sprinkle with cheese, salsa, tomato, green onions, and taco sauce.

2 Bake, uncovered, for 15 to 20 minutes or until heated through. Serve with tortilla chips or Veggie chips, if desired.

MAKES 32 (1/4-CUP) SERVINGS.

Janice Coffee
Wal-Mart *682   Rockvale, TN
Janice says that this dip is easy to make and that company will like it.

Olive-Nut Cheese Dip

ingredients

1 cup pimiento-stuffed green olives
1 pkg. (8 oz.) **Philadelphia® Cream Cheese**, softened
1/2 cup mayonnaise
1/2 cup chopped pecans
Assorted crackers

directions

1 Drain olives, reserving juice. Chop olives. In small bowl combine olives, 2 tablespoons of the reserved juice, cream cheese, mayonnaise, and pecans. Mix well. Cover and refrigerate for 8 to 24 hours.

2 Serve with crackers.

MAKES 20 (2-TABLESPOON) SERVINGS.

Cindy Isaacs
Wal-Mart *719   Berea, KY

According to Cindy, you can also shape this all-occasion dip into a ball or double the recipe for parties.

Pretzel Snacks

ingredients

1 tbsp. **McCormick® Dill Weed**
1 tbsp. **McCormick® Garlic Powder**
1 envelope (1 oz.) ranch salad dressing mix
2 lb. small pretzel twists
3/4 cup popcorn oil

directions

1 In small bowl stir together dill weed, garlic powder, and salad dressing mix.

2 In very large bowl combine pretzels and dill mixture. Drizzle with oil. Let stand for 6 to 8 hours, tossing occasionally.

MAKES 30 (3/4-CUP) SERVINGS.

Rita A. Barringer
Wal-Mart #1672   Ashland, WI
Rita received this recipe from a special family friend. It's served at holidays and large group gatherings.

Reuben Dip

ingredients

1 can (14 1/2 oz.) **Del Monte® Chopped Sauerkraut**, rinsed and well drained
12 oz. deli corned beef, chopped, or 1 can (12 oz.) corned beef
3/4 cup thousand island salad dressing
2 cups **Kraft® Shredded Swiss Cheese**
Pumpernickel party bread and/or rye crackers

directions

1 Preheat oven to 350°F. Spoon sauerkraut in bottom of 2-quart rectangular baking dish. Place corned beef over the top. Spread dressing over all. Sprinkle with cheese.

2 Bake, uncovered, about 20 minutes or until heated through.

3 Serve with bread and/or crackers.

MAKES 24 (2-TABLESPOON) SERVINGS.

Kathleen Uptagraw
Wal-Mart #1396   Baraboo, WI
Kathleen says you can add some mozzarella with the Swiss cheese if you like in this passed-on-from-a-friend favorite.

Spiced Tea

ingredients

2 sticks **McCormick® Cinnamon**, broken
1 tsp. **McCormick® Whole Cloves**
6 cups water
1 1/4 cups sugar
1 cup pineapple juice
1 cup orange juice
2 to 3 tbsp. lemon juice
6 bags tea

directions

1 Tie spices in cheesecloth bag. In large saucepan combine water, sugar, and spice bag. Bring to a boil; reduce heat. Cover and simmer at least 10 minutes. Remove and discard spice bag.

2 Stir in pineapple juice, orange juice, and lemon juice. Return to a boil. Add tea bags. Remove from heat. Cover and let stand for 10 minutes. Remove tea bags. Serve warm or chilled.

MAKES 10 (6-OUNCE) SERVINGS.

Cynda Crimmins
Wal-Mart *711   Glasgow, KY
Cynda's mother makes this recipe in the fall when there is a chill in the air. The children in the family enjoy it after a night of Halloween fun.

Sweet and Sour Meatballs

ingredients

1 egg, slightly beaten
1/2 cup crushed saltine crackers
1/4 cup finely chopped onion
1/4 cup milk
1/2 tsp. each **McCormick® Garlic Salt** and **Ground Black Pepper**
1/4 tsp. salt
1 lb. lean ground beef
3/4 cup ketchup
1/4 cup vinegar
1/3 cup packed brown sugar
3 tbsp. yellow mustard

directions

1 Preheat oven to 350°F. For meatballs, in medium bowl combine egg, crackers, onion, milk, garlic salt, pepper, and salt. Add beef; mix well. Shape into 1-inch balls. Place meatballs in a 15x10x1-inch baking pan.

2 Bake for 15 to 18 minutes or until an instant-read thermometer inserted into center of a meatball registers 160°F.

3 Using a slotted spoon, transfer meatballs to large saucepan or Dutch oven. In small bowl stir together ketchup, vinegar, brown sugar, and mustard. Pour over meatballs. Cook over low heat until heated through. Transfer to a serving bowl. Serve with toothpicks.

MAKES 12 SERVINGS.

Teresa Miller
Wal-Mart #1433   Celina, OH
Teresa likes to make these yummy meatballs for family gatherings. While they're baking, other dishes can be prepared.

Vegetable Dip

ingredients

1 carton (16 oz.) sour cream
1 1/2 cups mayonnaise or salad dressing
2 tbsp. **McCormick® Season-All®**
    Seasoned Salt
5 tsp. Worcestershire sauce
1 tbsp. **McCormick® Minced Onions**
1 tbsp. **McCormick® Parsley Flakes**
1 tsp. **McCormick® Dill Seed**
Assorted cut-up vegetables or crackers

directions

1 In medium bowl stir together sour cream, mayonnaise, seasoned salt, Worcestershire sauce, onions, parsley, and dill seed. Cover and refrigerate at least 2 hours.

2 Serve with vegetables or crackers.

MAKES 15 (4-TABLESPOON) SERVINGS.

Cathy Midtgard
Wal-Mart *1809 Reading, MI
Cathy says, "This is a great dip for all vegetables and crackers."

Veggie Dip of the Gods

ingredients

2 cups mayonnaise

3 green onions, trimmed and cut into
    1-inch pieces

1/2 of a can (2 oz.) anchovy fillets, drained
    (6 fillets)

1 tbsp. lemon juice

1 tbsp. **McCormick® Parsley Flakes**

1/2 to 1 1/2 tsp. **McCormick® Bottled
    Fresh Garlic**

Assorted fresh vegetables

directions

1 In blender or food processor combine
mayonnaise, green onions, anchovies,
lemon juice, parsley flakes, and garlic.
Cover and blend or process until smooth.
Transfer mixture to a small bowl. Cover
and refrigerate for 2 hours.

2 Serve with assorted vegetables.

MAKES 18 (2-TABLESPOON) SERVINGS.

Lynne McClave
Wal-Mart *923   Noblesville, IN
*Lynne says that the anchovies
are the secret ingredient in the tasty
dip, and people who swear they
dislike anchovies love this dip.*

Warm Crab Dip

ingredients

2 pkg. (8 oz. each) **Philadelphia® Cream Cheese**, softened
1 tsp. **McCormick® Ground Mustard**
1 tsp. prepared horseradish
1 tsp. Worcestershire sauce
1 medium onion, finely chopped
1 lb. cooked fresh crabmeat or imitation crabmeat chunks
1/2 cup slivered almonds
Thin wheat crackers and/or vegetable-flavored crackers

directions

1 Preheat oven to 350°F. In large bowl stir together cream cheese, mustard, horseradish, and Worcestershire sauce. Stir in onion until combined. Gently stir in crabmeat. Spread in bottom of 2-quart rectangular baking dish. Sprinkle with almonds.

2 Bake for 30 minutes or until almonds are toasted and mixture is heated through. Serve with crackers.

MAKES 20 (3-TABLESPOON) SERVINGS.

Mary Lee Gehret
Wal-Mart #1331 Sidney, OH
This recipe is from Mary Lee's sister, who lives on an inlet near the Chesapeake Bay. It's a treat when she serves it with fresh crabmeat at the family reunion.

Barbecued Chicken Pizza

ingredients

2 pkg. (8 oz. each) refrigerated crescent rolls

3 skinless, boneless chicken breast halves, cooked and chopped

1/2 cup sliced fresh mushrooms

1/2 cup chopped onion

1/2 cup chopped green bell pepper

1/4 cup sliced pitted ripe olives

1 cup hickory smoke barbecue sauce

1 cup **Kraft® Shredded Low Moisture Part-Skim Mozzarella Cheese**

1 cup **Kraft® Finely Shredded Cheddar Cheese**

1/4 cup **Kraft® 100% Grated Parmesan Cheese**

directions

1 Preheat oven to 375°F. Unroll crescent roll dough on baking sheet. Pinch seams together and press dough into a 15x10 rectangle, building up edges.

2 Top dough with chicken, mushrooms, onion, bell pepper, (if desired, cook onion and bell pepper in 2 teaspoons cooking oil until tender), and olives. Drizzle barbecue sauce over all. Sprinkle with cheeses.

3 Bake about 20 minutes or until crust is golden brown and cheese is melted.

SERVES 8.

Virginia A. Lane
Wal-Mart #1318   Knoxville, TN
To save on time, Virginia suggests using a packaged prebaked pizza crust and precooked chicken. Add a salad and dinner is ready in less than 30 minutes.

Beef and Bean Cornbread Bake

ingredients

2 lb. ground beef
1 small onion, chopped
1 small green bell pepper, chopped
3 cans (16 oz.) **BUSH'S® BEST Great
   Northern Beans**, drained
1 can (14 1/2 oz.) **Del Monte® Diced
   Tomatoes**
1 can (10 3/4 oz.) cream of celery soup
1/4 tsp. **McCormick® Garlic Powder**
1/4 tsp. **McCormick® Ground Black Pepper**
1 pkg. (8 1/2 oz.) corn muffin mix

directions

1 Preheat oven to 350°F. In 4-quart
Dutch oven cook beef, onion, and bell
pepper, half at a time, until beef is brown;
drain fat. Return ground beef mixture to
Dutch oven.

2 Stir beans, undrained tomatoes, soup,
garlic powder, and black pepper into beef
mixture. Bring to a boil. Pour into greased
13x9x2-inch baking pan.

3 Prepare corn muffin mix according
to package directions. Spoon over bean
mixture, pushing batter down into beans
with handle of wooden spoon.

4 Bake, uncovered, for 30 to 45 minutes
or until golden brown. Let stand for 10 to
15 minutes before cutting into squares
to serve.

SERVES 12.

James Wilder
Wal-Mart #1289   Wilmington, OH
*James always receives compliments
on this casserole when he takes it to
the men's fellowship at his church.*

Cajun Breakfast

Tom's Hudspeth
Wal-Mart *672   Maryville, TN
This recipe was a breakfast favorite of Thomas when he was growing up in Louisiana. Now his 16-year-old son requests the dish.

ingredients

4 eggs
1/2 cup milk
1/2 tsp. salt
1/2 to 1 tsp. **McCormick® Ground Black Pepper**
1/2 to 1 tsp. **McCormick® Crushed Red Pepper Flakes**
1/2 of a link (8 oz.) cooked smoked sausage, halved lengthwise and sliced*
1 red, green, or yellow bell pepper, chopped
1 medium onion, chopped
4 green onions, chopped
1 tbsp. **McCormick® Bottled Fresh Garlic**
2 tbsp. **Enova™ Oil**
6 cups cooked **Mahatma® White Rice**

directions

1 In medium bowl whisk together eggs, milk, salt, black pepper, and crushed red pepper until combined; set aside.

2 In 12-inch skillet cook sausage, bell pepper, onion, half of the green onions, and garlic in hot oil until onion is tender and sausage starts to brown, about 4 minutes.

3 Add rice to skillet; spread in an even layer. Cook over medium heat, stirring occasionally, until rice is browned, about 5 minutes. Add egg mixture. Cook, stirring gently, until egg mixture appears set, about 1 to 2 minutes.

4 Transfer to serving dish. Garnish with remaining green onions.

Note: Substitute cooked diced ham or cooked, peeled, and deveined shrimp for the sausage, if desired.

SERVES 4 TO 6.

Calico Beans

ingredients

1 lb. ground beef
1 large onion, chopped
1 lb. bacon, chopped
1 can (16 oz.) **BUSH'S® BEST Dark Red Kidney Beans**, rinsed and drained
1 can (16 oz.) **BUSH'S® BEST Large Butter Beans**, rinsed and drained
1 can (16 oz.) **BUSH'S® BEST Pinto Beans**, rinsed and drained
1 can (14 1/2 oz.) **Del Monte® Lima Beans**, rinsed and drained
1 1/2 cups ketchup
3/4 cup packed brown sugar
2 tbsp. vinegar
2 tbsp. Worcestershire sauce
1 tbsp. **McCormick® Ground Mustard**
1/2 tsp. salt

directions

1 In large skillet cook beef and onion until beef is brown; drain fat. Transfer beef mixture to a 3 1/2- to 4-quart slow cooker. In same skillet cook bacon until crisp. Drain bacon, discarding drippings. Add bacon to slow cooker. Add beans, ketchup, brown sugar, vinegar, Worcestershire sauce, mustard, and salt to slow cooker. Stir to combine.

2 Cover and cook on low-heat setting for 6 to 8 hours or on high-heat setting for 3 to 4 hours.

SERVES 6 TO 8.

Pat Weseli
Wal-Mart #1446   Rice Lake, WI
Pat likes to make this recipe for picnics or Wal-Mart parties because it makes a big pot of beans. You can vary the type of beans to suit your taste.

Cheesy Hamburger Hash Brown Casserole

ingredients

1 lb. ground beef
1/2 cup chopped onion
2 tsp. **McCormick® Garlic Powder**
1 tsp. **McCormick® Chili Powder**
3/4 tsp. **McCormick® Lemon & Pepper Seasoning Salt**
3/4 tsp. **McCormick® Season-All® Seasoned Salt**
1/2 of a pkg. (30 oz.) frozen **Ore-Ida® Country Style Hash Browns**
2 cups **Kraft® Shredded Cheddar Cheese**
1 can (10 3/4 oz.) cream of chicken soup
1 carton (16 oz.) sour cream

directions

1 Preheat oven to 350°F. In large skillet cook beef and onion until beef is brown; drain fat. Stir in garlic powder, chili powder, lemon and pepper seasoning salt, and seasoned salt. Cook and stir 1 minute more.

2 In very large bowl stir together hash browns, 1 cup of the cheese, soup, and sour cream until combined. Stir in ground beef mixture.

3 Transfer mixture to 3-quart rectangular baking dish. Bake, uncovered, for 30 minutes. Top with remaining cheese and bake about 15 minutes more or until heated through.

SERVES 8.

Edna Broshears
Wal-Mart *566 Booneville, IN
This recipe is great for family get-togethers or just a quiet dinner at home, according to Edna.

Chicken and Mushroom Pasta Bake

Viola Spalding
Wal-Mart #2691   Corydon, IN
*Viola has fond memories of having
this for dinner on Sunday.*

ingredients

3 lb. meaty chicken pieces
1 medium onion, cut up
1 jar (24 oz.) **Bertolli® Tomato & Basil Sauce**
1 can (4 oz.) sliced mushrooms
1/4 tsp. salt
1/8 tsp. **McCormick® Ground Black Pepper**
16 oz. rotini pasta
1 lb. **Velveeta® Pasteurized Prepared Cheese
     Product**, cut into cubes and softened
1/2 cup **Kraft® 100% Grated Parmesan Cheese**
Kraft® 100% Grated Parmesan Cheese (optional)

directions

1 Place chicken and onion in 6- to 8-quart Dutch
oven. Add just enough water to cover. Bring to
a boil; reduce heat. Simmer, covered, 15 to
20 minutes or until chicken is no longer pink.
Remove chicken; reserve broth. Let chicken
stand until cool enough to handle; discard skin
and bones. Coarsely shred chicken.

2 Strain broth; return 2 cups to pan. Discard
remaining broth. Add sauce, undrained
mushrooms, salt, and pepper to broth. Bring to a
boil; reduce heat. Simmer, uncovered, 10 minutes.
Stir in chicken.

3 Preheat oven to 350°F. Meanwhile, cook
rotini according to package directions; drain. In
3-quart rectangular baking dish place half of the
rotini. Top with half of the cheeses and half of
the chicken mixture. Repeat layers. If desired,
sprinkle with additional Parmesan cheese.

4 Bake, uncovered, for 30 to 40 minutes or
until mixture is heated through. Let stand
10 minutes before serving.

SERVES 8 TO 10.

Chicken Chowder

Nancye Hoganson
Wal-Mart *3209   Elk River, MN
Nancye likes to make this soup on bitterly cold Minnesota nights. It's a hearty soup to come home to. Nancye serves it with crusty garlic bread.

ingredients

6 slices bacon, chopped
1 lb. skinless, boneless chicken breast halves, cut into 1-inch pieces
1/2 cup each chopped celery and thinly sliced carrot
1/4 cup sliced green onion
1 tsp. **McCormick® Paprika**
1/2 tsp. salt
2 cups prepared **Ore-Ida® Mashed Potatoes**
2 cups half-and-half or light cream
1 can (14 3/4 oz.) **Del Monte® Cream Style Golden Sweet Corn**
1 cup **Kraft® Shredded Cheddar Cheese**
1/2 cup frozen green peas
McCormick® Course Grind Black Pepper

directions

1 In 4-quart Dutch oven cook bacon over medium heat until crisp. Drain bacon, reserving drippings. Cook chicken in drippings for 4 to 6 minutes or until chicken is no longer pink, stirring occasionally. Remove chicken from pan.

2 Add celery, carrot, and green onion to pan. Cook about 5 minutes or until vegetables are tender, stirring occasionally. Stir in paprika and salt. Add potatoes, half-and-half, corn, cheese, and peas. Cook and stir over medium-low heat until cheese is melted. Return chicken to pan. Heat through. Top each serving with cooked bacon and sprinkle with pepper.

SERVES 6.

Crunchy Catfish Fillets

ingredients

2 eggs, slightly beaten
1/4 cup milk
1 cup packaged instant mashed potato flakes
1/2 cup buttermilk self-rising cornmeal mix
1 tsp. **McCormick® Season-All® Seasoned Salt**
Dash **McCormick® Cayenne Pepper** (optional)
2 cups **Enova™ Oil**
4 catfish fillets (thaw, if frozen)

directions

1 In shallow dish combine eggs and milk. In another shallow dish combine potato flakes, cornmeal mix, seasoned salt, and cayenne pepper (if desired).

2 Heat oil in large deep skillet. Dip fish in egg mixture then roll in potato flake mixture. Dip again in egg mixture. Coat again with potato flake mixture. Cook in hot oil about 8 minutes or until golden brown and fish flakes with a fork, turning once.

SERVES 4.

Fayme Bullock
Wal-Mart *1165 Irvington, KY
This recipe reminds Fayme of family fishing trips when they always caught enough catfish to feed a small army.

Crunchy Skillet Dinner

ingredients

1 bag **Success® Boil-in-Bag Brown Rice**
1 lb. fully cooked smoked sausage, cut into
 1-inch pieces
1 medium onion, coarsely chopped
1 tbsp. **Enova™ Oil**
1 1/3 cups water
1 can (10 3/4 oz.) cream of mushroom soup
1/2 cup diagonally sliced celery
1/2 cup frozen peas
1/2 cup chow mein noodles

directions

1 Cook rice according to package directions. Set aside.

2 In large skillet cook sausage and onion in oil until sausage is brown and onion is tender. Stir in cooked rice, water, soup, and celery. Bring to a boil; reduce heat. Simmer, uncovered, for 15 minutes, stirring occasionally. Stir in peas. Simmer, uncovered, for 3 to 4 minutes more or until heated through.

3 Transfer to a serving bowl. Sprinkle with noodles.

SERVES 6.

Linda McGarrity
Wal-Mart #477   Soddy-Daisy, TN
There is no heating up the oven when Linda serves this tasty meal to family and guests.

Dad's Best Lasagna

David Southard
Wal-Mart *1836   Riga, MI
David likes to cook and he says it's a great hobby for him. This lasagna is one of his family's favorites.

ingredients

8 oz. lasagna noodles (9 noodles)
1 lb. ground beef
1 cup each finely chopped onion and finely chopped green bell pepper
1 jar (24 oz.) **Bertolli® Tomato & Basil Sauce**
1 carton (16 oz.) cottage cheese, drained
1 can (14 1/2 oz.) **Del Monte® Diced Tomatoes**, drained
1 can (8 oz.) mushroom stems and pieces, drained
1/4 tsp. **McCormick® Garlic Powder**
2 cups **Kraft® Shredded Low Moisture Part-Skim Mozzarella Cheese**

directions

1 Preheat oven to 350°F. Coat 3-quart rectangular baking dish with nonstick cooking spray; set aside. Cook lasagna noodles according to package directions. Drain; set aside. In 12-inch skillet cook beef, onion, and bell pepper until beef is brown and vegetables are tender; drain fat. Stir in sauce, cottage cheese, tomatoes, mushrooms, and garlic powder. Heat until mixture just reaches a simmer.

2 Spread 1 cup of the sauce mixture in bottom of prepared dish. Top with 3 noodles. Top with one-third of the remaining sauce mixture. Top with 3 more noodles, one-third remaining sauce mixture, remaining noodles, and remaining sauce. Sprinkle with cheese, being sure to cover edges of noodles.

3 Bake, uncovered, for 30 minutes or until hot and bubbly.

SERVES 12.

Don's Deep-Dish Pizza

Don Gregory
Wal-Mart #2818   Crown Point, IN
*Don likes to reserve a few of the
vegetables and some cheese to sprinkle
on the last few minutes of baking.*

ingredients

Crust

3 cups **Kraft® Shredded Low Moisture
  Part-Skim Mozzarella Cheese**
1 pkg. (3 1/2 oz.) sliced pepperoni
1 cup each chopped onion, chopped
  green bell pepper, and thinly sliced
  fresh mushrooms
1 can (2 1/4 oz.) sliced pitted ripe olives,
  drained
1 jar (24 oz.) **Bertolli® Tomato & Basil
  Sauce**
1 to 2 tbsp. **Enova™ Oil**

directions

1 Prepare crust. Preheat oven to 375°F.
Punch dough down. Knead on floured
surface for 2 minutes. Roll dough into
16-inch circle; transfer to greased 14-inch
pizza pan, allowing dough to hang over edge.

2 Sprinkle cheese in center of dough,
leaving a 4-inch border. Top with pepperoni,
onion, bell pepper, mushrooms, olives, and
sauce. Fold dough over toppings. Brush
crust with oil. Bake 45 to 50 minutes or
until crust is golden brown. Let stand on
rack 10 minutes.

Crust: In bowl stir together 1 3/4 cups warm
water, 2 packages yeast, and 1 teaspoon
sugar until dissolved. Let stand 5 minutes.
Add 1/3 cup **Enova™ Oil**, 1 1/2 teaspoon
salt, and 1/4 teaspoon **McCormick® Garlic
Powder**. Stir in 4 1/2 cups of flour. On
floured surface, knead in enough flour
(1/2 to 1 cup) to make a moderately soft
dough (6 to 8 minutes). Cover; let rise
until nearly double (about 1 hour).

SERVES 8.

Easy Brown Butter Pasta with Chicken

Heather N. Zernich
Wal-Mart *1707   East Liverpool, OH
Heather says, "The richness of the butter sauce with fresh parsley, herbs, lemon, and melted mozzarella is very satisfying."

ingredients

1 cup chicken broth
1/2 tsp. **McCormick® Rosemary Leaves**
2 tbsp. **McCormick® Rubbed Sage**
4 large skinless, boneless chicken breast halves
2 tbsp. Merlot or chicken broth
1 cup unsalted butter
McCormick® Gourmet Collection® Black Peppercorns Grinder
1 pkg. (20 oz.) refrigerated herb chicken tortellini or cheese tortellini, cooked
1 cup chopped fresh parsley
3/4 cup **Kraft® Shredded Low Moisture Part-Skim Mozzarella Cheese**
1 to 2 tbsp. lemon juice

directions

1 In large nonstick skillet mix 1/2 cup of the broth, rosemary, and 1 teaspoon of the sage; cook chicken in broth mixture over medium heat for 15 to 20 minutes or until chicken is no longer pink. If necessary, carefully add a little water during cooking.

2 Meanwhile, in small saucepan combine butter and reamaining sage. Heat over low heat until butter melts and turns delicate brown, stirring constantly. Set aside.

3 Remove chicken from skillet. Keep warm. Add wine or broth to skillet, stirring to scrape up any browned bits. Stir in browned butter and remaining 1/2 cup broth. Bring to a boil; reduce heat. Simmer 5 minutes. Season to taste with pepper.

4 Pour half of butter mixture over tortellini. Add parsley, cheese, and lemon juice. Toss to combine. Serve topped with chicken and remaining butter mixture.

SERVES 4.

Excellent Chili

ingredients

1 lb. lean ground beef
1 small onion, chopped
1 small green bell pepper, chopped
2 cans (14 1/2 oz. each) **Del Monte®
Stewed Tomatoes with Onions,
Celery & Green Peppers**, cut up
2 cans (16 oz.) **BUSH'S® BEST Chili Beans**
2 cans (10 3/4 oz. each) tomato soup
1 can (15 oz.) **Del Monte® Tomato Sauce**
1 1/2 tsp. **McCormick® Chili Powder**
Corn tortilla chips (optional)

directions

1 In large skillet cook beef, onion, and bell pepper until beef is brown and vegetables are tender. Drain fat.

2 In 5- to 6-quart Dutch oven combine undrained tomatoes, undrained chili beans, soup, 2 2/3 cups water, tomato sauce, and chili powder. Bring to a boil; add ground beef mixture. Reduce heat. Cover and gently simmer for 1 hour, stirring occasionally.

3 Serve over tortilla chips (if desired).

SERVES 9 TO 12.

Donna Lynne Walkerow
Wal-Mart *1812   Wooster, OH
On a cold winter day, Donna serves her family bowls of steaming hot chili accompanied by grilled cheese sandwiches.

Heather's Hearty Chicken

ingredients

4 medium skinless, boneless chicken breast halves

1 jar (24 oz.) **Bertolli® Tomato & Basil Sauce**

2 cups **Kraft® Shredded Low Moisture Part-Skim Mozzarella Cheese**

1 cup sliced fresh mushrooms

2 tbsp. **Kraft® 100% Grated Parmesan Cheese**

Hot cooked pasta

directions

1 Preheat oven to 400°F. Arrange chicken in 2-quart rectangular baking dish. Spoon sauce over chicken. Sprinkle with 1 cup of the mozzarella cheese, mushrooms, and Parmesan cheese.

2 Bake, uncovered, for 20 minutes. Sprinkle with remaining mozzarella cheese. Bake for 10 to 15 minutes more or until chicken is no longer pink. Serve with hot cooked pasta.

SERVES 4.

Heather Howell Tatum
Wal-Mart #1675   Lebanon, KY
Round out the meal with a vegetable and a crisp green salad and dinner is ready in less than an hour.

Jill's Favorite Eggs

ingredients

4 slices bacon
6 eggs
1/4 cup sour cream
1 1/2 tsp. **McCormick® Gourmet Collection® Greek Seasoning**
1 can (4 oz.) sliced mushrooms, drained
4 oz. **Kraft® American Cheese**, cubed

directions

1 In large skillet cook bacon until crisp. Remove to paper towels to drain. Drain fat from skillet; wipe out skillet and set aside. When cool, crumble bacon.

2 In large bowl whisk together eggs, sour cream, and seasoning until smooth. Stir in crumbled bacon, mushrooms, and cheese.

3 Lightly coat the skillet with nonstick cooking spray. Heat skillet over medium heat. Add egg mixture. Cook until set, lifting cooked portions to allow uncooked portion to flow underneath. Remove from heat and let stand 5 minutes until cheese melts.

SERVES 4 TO 6.

April J. Feinberg
Wal-Mart #1819   Menomonie, WI
When April was growing up, she and her sister Jill enjoyed making this breakfast together. When visiting her sister, April still makes this recipe.

Kielbasa and Shrimp Creole

Wanda Lee
Wal-Mart #738 Big Sandy, TN
*Wanda's family likes spicy foods and
this recipe is one of their favorites.
It's delicious as well as quick
and easy to prepare.*

ingredients

1 cup **Mahatma® White Rice**
4 oz. fully-cooked kielbasa, sliced
1/2 cup chopped onion
1/4 cup chopped green bell pepper
1/4 cup chopped celery
1 tsp. **McCormick® Cajun Seasoning**
1/4 tsp. salt
1/4 tsp. **McCormick® Cayenne Pepper**
1/4 tsp. **McCormick® Ground Black
    Pepper**
1 tbsp. **Enova™ Oil**
1 can (14 1/2 oz.) **Del Monte® Diced
    Tomatoes with Garlic & Onion**
1/2 lb. peeled and deveined large shrimp
    (thaw, if frozen)

directions

1 Cook rice according to package
directions. Keep warm.

2 In large nonstick skillet cook kielbasa,
onion, bell pepper, celery, Cajun seasoning,
salt, cayenne pepper, and black pepper in
hot oil about 4 minutes or until vegetables
are tender.

3 Stir in undrained tomatoes. Bring to a
boil; reduce heat. Simmer, uncovered, for
2 minutes. Stir in shrimp. Cook, stirring
occasionally, over medium heat for 2 to
3 minutes or until shrimp turn opaque.
Serve over hot cooked rice.

SERVES 4.

Kylie's Vegetarian Baked Ziti

Kylie Hatmaker
Wal-Mart *2065   Knoxville, TN
Kylie makes this quick meal about once a week for her family. It's a great-tasting meal that's easy to prepare.

ingredients

12 oz. ziti or mostaccioli
2 tbsp. **Enova™ Oil**
1 jar (24 oz.) **Bertolli® Tomato & Basil Sauce, Roasted Red Pepper Sauce,** or **Olive Oil and Garlic Sauce**
1 container (15 oz.) part-skim ricotta cheese
2 cups **Kraft® Shredded Low Moisture Part-Skim Mozzarella Cheese**
3/4 cup **Kraft® 100% Grated Parmesan Cheese**

directions

1 Preheat oven to 350°F. In large saucepan cook ziti according to package directions, adding oil to the cooking water; drain. Return ziti to saucepan. Gently stir in sauce, ricotta cheese, 1 1/2 cups of the mozzarella cheese, and Parmesan.

2 Spoon into 2-quart rectangular baking dish. Top with remaining 1/2 cup mozzarella. Bake for 25 to 30 minutes or until heated through.

SERVES 6.

Loretta's Meat Loaf

ingredients

1 can (8 oz.) **Contadina® Tomato Sauce**
1/4 cup light-colored corn syrup
2 tbsp. yellow mustard
1 cup finely chopped, peeled, cored
    apples
2 eggs, slightly beaten
1/2 cup fine dry bread crumbs
1/2 cup chopped onion
1 tsp. salt
1/2 tsp. **McCormick® Ground Nutmeg**
1/8 tsp. **McCormick® Ground Black**
    Pepper
1 1/2 lb. lean ground beef

directions

1 Preheat oven to 350°F. In small bowl
stir together tomato sauce, corn syrup,
and mustard. In large bowl stir together
3/4 cup of the tomato sauce mixture,
apples, eggs, bread crumbs, onion, salt,
nutmeg, and pepper until well combined.
Add ground beef; mix well.

2 Coat 2-quart rectangular baking dish
with nonstick cooking spray. Place meat in
dish and shape into 8x4x2-inch loaf.

3 Bake, uncovered, for 30 minutes. Pour
remaining tomato sauce mixture atop loaf.
Bake for 30 to 45 minutes more or until
internal temperature registers 160°F.
Spoon off fat. Let stand 10 minutes
before serving.

SERVES 6 TO 8.

Loretta Jackson
Wal-Mart #2783   Lexington, KY
*This family-favorite recipe of Loretta's is
juicy from the apple. She sometimes
doubles the recipe to make two loaves.*

Nancy's Special Chicken Salad

ingredients

4 large chicken breast halves with bone
2 cans (14 oz. each) chicken broth
3 ribs celery, finely chopped
4 green onions, thinly sliced
1 1/2 cups light mayonnaise
1 tbsp. **McCormick® Tarragon Leaves**
1/2 tsp. **McCormick® Ground White Pepper**
1 can (20 oz.) **Del Monte® Pineapple Tidbits In Its Own Juice**, drained
1 cup chopped walnuts, toasted
Lettuce leaves

directions

1 Place chicken and broth in 4-quart Dutch oven. Bring to a boil; reduce heat. Cover and simmer for 50 to 60 minutes or until chicken is no longer pink. Remove chicken to a large bowl to cool; reserve broth.

2 When chicken is cool enough to handle, discard skin and bones. Use 2 forks to shred chicken. Place in large bowl.

3 Add celery, onions, mayonnaise, tarragon, pepper, and 1/2 cup reserved broth to chicken. Stir to combine. Stir in pineapple and walnuts.

4 Cover and refrigerate for 4 to 24 hours. Serve on lettuce leaves.

SERVES 10 TO 12.

Nancy B. Osterhout
Wal-Mart *1479   Valparaiso, IN
Nancy has shared this recipe with friends and family and it's become a favorite. She dresses up the salad with pineapple and walnuts.

Nanie's Lasagna

Sharon Schmidt
Wal-Mart #698   Cleveland, TN
*The recipe name came from Sharon's
granddaughters who call her Nanie.
They call the recipe Nanie's Zonya, because
the girls couldn't pronounce lasagna.*

ingredients

8 oz. lasagna noodles
1 tbsp. **Enova™ Oil**
1 lb. ground beef
1 lb. bulk hot Italian sausage or sweet
    Italian sausage
2 jars (24 oz. each) **Bertolli® Marinara
    with Burgundy Wine** or **Tomato &
    Basil Sauce**
1 tsp. **McCormick® Italian Seasoning**
8 oz. **Kraft® Mozzarella Cheese Slices**,
    torn into strips
8 oz. **Kraft® Pepperjack Cheese Slices**
    or **Mozzarella Cheese Slices**, torn
    into strips

directions

1 Preheat oven to 350°F. Cook noodles
according to package directions, adding
oil to cooking water. Drain.

2 In 4- to 6-quart Dutch oven cook meat,
half at a time, until brown; drain fat. Return
all meat to pan. Stir in sauce, Italian
seasoning, and salt and pepper to taste.
Bring mixture to a boil over medium heat;
reduce heat. Simmer, covered, over low
heat about 45 minutes, stirring frequently.

3 In 3-quart rectangular baking dish
spread about 2 cups of the meat sauce.
Layer half of the noodles on the sauce,
then half of the cheese pieces. Repeat
with half of the remaining sauce, remaining
noodles, remaining cheese, then remaining
sauce.

4 Bake, uncovered, about 30 to
35 minutes or until bubbly. Let stand
10 minutes before serving.

SERVES 8.

Neapolitan Eggplant Bake

Anita P. Warwick
Wal-Mart *3529   Indianapolis, IN
A taste of tradition made new—Anita updated her mother's recipe brought from Italy by using packaged ingredients readily available in today's supermarkets.

ingredients

2 eggs

3 small eggplants, peeled and cut into 1/4-inch-thick slices (about 2 lb.)

1 1/2 cups plain or seasoned fine dry bread crumbs

2 jars (24 oz. each) **Bertolli® Tomato & Basil Sauce**

2 tbsp. **Enova™ Oil**

1 1/2 tsp. **McCormick® Garlic Powder**

4 cups **Kraft® Shredded Low Moisture Part-Skim Mozzarella Cheese**

1/2 cup **Kraft® 100% Grated Parmesan Cheese**

1/2 tsp. **McCormick® Basil Leaves**

directions

1 Preheat oven to 350°F. In shallow bowl beat eggs. Dip eggplant slices into eggs, then into bread crumbs, turning to coat both sides. Place slices on 2 large baking sheets. Bake for 15 to 20 minutes or until golden brown, turning slices once during baking.

2 Spread 2 cups of the sauce in bottom of 3-quart rectangular baking dish. Place one-third of the eggplant slices on top of sauce in dish. Sprinkle with 2 teaspoons of the oil and 1/2 teaspoon of the garlic powder. Top with one-third each of mozzarella and Parmesan cheeses. Repeat layers 2 more times using remaining sauce, eggplant, oil, garlic powder, and cheeses. Sprinkle basil over top.

3 Bake, uncovered, about 35 minutes or until heated through.

SERVES 8 TO 10.

Old-Fashioned Lasagna

ingredients

1 pkg. (16 oz.) lasagna noodles
1 lb. ground beef
1 medium onion, chopped
2 cloves garlic, minced
2 cans (6 oz. each) **Del Monte® Tomato Paste**
1 tbsp. **McCormick® Parsley Flakes**
2 tsp. **McCormick® Basil**
1 tsp. **McCormick® Oregano**
   (optional)
1/8 tsp. salt
1 cup ricotta cheese
2 eggs, beaten
2 cups **Kraft® Shredded Low Moisture Part-Skim**
   Mozzarella Cheese
1/4 cup **Kraft® 100% Grated Parmesan Cheese**

directions

1 Preheat oven to 350°F. Cook lasagna noodles according to package directions. Drain; set aside.

2 In large skillet cook beef, onion, and garlic until beef is brown; drain fat. Stir in tomato paste, 2 cups water, parsley, basil, oregano (if desired), and salt. Cover and simmer over medium-high heat for 10 minutes. In bowl combine ricotta cheese and eggs.

3 In 13x9x2-inch baking pan place a thin layer of meat mixture. Top with half of the noodles. Spread all of the ricotta mixture over noodles. Top with half of the mozzarella and half of the meat sauce. Layer with remaining noodles, remaining meat sauce, and remaining mozzarella. Sprinkle Parmesan on top.

4 Cover with foil and bake for 35 to 40 minutes or until heated through. Let stand 10 minutes before serving.

SERVES 6 TO 8.

Barbara Browning
Wal-Mart *1140   Mt. Sterling, KY
"I've been making this recipe for so long I don't remember who gave it to me. I'm often asked to make it for fund-raising lunches at work," according to Barbara.

Pepper Casserole

Deb Stearns
Wal-Mart *5355   Kenton, OH
Deb's family loves stuffed peppers but you only get one color pepper, so she came up with this recipe. It's a little easier to make and you get a different color of pepper with every bite.

ingredients

1 bag **Success® Boil-In-Bag White Rice**
4 bell peppers (red, green, yellow, and/or orange), cut into strips
1/4 cup water
1 lb. ground beef
1 lb. bulk sweet or hot Italian sausage
1 small onion, cut into wedges
1 tsp. **McCormick® Italian Seasoning**
1/2 tsp. salt
1/2 to 1 tsp. **McCormick® Ground Black Pepper**
2 tbsp. **Kraft® 100% Grated Parmesan Cheese**
1 1/2 cups **Kraft® Shredded Low Moisture Part-Skim Mozzarella Cheese**

directions

1 Preheat oven to 350°F. Cook rice according to package directions.

2 Meanwhile, place bell peppers in 2-quart rectangular baking dish. Add water; set aside.

3 In 12-inch skillet cook beef, sausage, and onion, half at a time, until meat is brown, breaking up large pieces; drain fat. Stir in cooked rice, Italian seasoning, salt, black pepper, Parmesan, and 2 tablespoons of the mozzarella. Spoon over peppers in dish. Top with remaining mozzarella. Cover loosely with foil.

4 Bake for 30 to 40 minutes or until peppers are tender.

SERVES 6 TO 8.

Pepper Steak

Michelle Hrnyak
Wal-Mart #2073   Cleveland, OH
This recipe is a favorite of Michelle's because it was her grandpa's specialty. He takes it to family potlucks and although Michelle has tweaked it a bit, it's still his recipe.

ingredients

3 lb. beef round steak, cut into 1/2-inch-wide, bite-size strips

2 tbsp. **Enova™ Oil**

2 cans (10 3/4 oz. each) cream of mushroom soup

1 1/2 cups water

1/2 cup soy sauce

2 tbsp. **SPLENDA® No Calorie Sweetener, Granular**

3 medium green bell peppers, cut into strips

2 medium onions, halved lengthwise and thinly sliced

1 can (8 oz.) water chestnuts, drained (optional)

1 can (4 oz.) sliced mushrooms, drained (optional)

6 cups cooked **Carolina® White Rice**

directions

1 In 4-quart Dutch oven cook steak strips, half at a time, in hot oil until brown. Return all steak strips to pan.

2 In large bowl combine mushroom soup, water, soy sauce, and sweetener. Pour over meat in pan. Bring to a boil; reduce heat. Simmer, covered, for 45 minutes or until meat is tender. Stir in bell peppers, onions, water chestnuts, and mushrooms (if desired). Simmer, covered, for 20 minutes more or until steak and vegetables are tender. Serve over rice.

SERVES 8.

Potato-Crusted Meat Pie

Julie Hollenbeck
Wal-Mart *3624 Monticello, MN
Julie and her mother created this recipe for the men in their lives. As it turned out, everyone loves the recipe. It makes a great meal for a chilly fall day.

ingredients

1 egg, lightly beaten
1 1/2 cups frozen **Ore-Ida® Country Style Hash Browns**, partially thawed
3/4 cup **Kraft® Shredded Parmesan Cheese**
1 lb. ground beef
1/2 cup each chopped onion and chopped celery
1 can (15 oz.) **Del Monte® Tomato Sauce**
1 cup **Kraft® Finely Shredded Cheddar Cheese**
1 can (4 oz.) sliced mushrooms, drained
1/2 cup sliced pimiento-stuffed green olives
1/2 tsp. salt
1/2 tsp. **McCormick® Ground Black Pepper**
1/4 to 1/2 tsp. **McCormick® Oregano Leaves**

directions

1 Preheat oven to 400°F. In large bowl stir together egg, potatoes, and Parmesan cheese. Press onto bottom and sides of greased 2-quart casserole. Set aside.

2 In large skillet cook beef, onion, and celery until meat is brown. Drain fat. Stir in tomato sauce, Cheddar cheese, mushrooms, olives, salt, pepper, and oregano. Pour into potato crust. Sprinkle with additional shredded Cheddar cheese, if desired.

3 Bake for 35 to 40 minutes or until heated through. Let stand for 10 minutes before serving.

SERVES 6 TO 8.

Potato-Topped Casserole

ingredients

1 lb. lean ground beef
1/2 cup chopped onion
1/2 tsp. salt
1/4 tsp. **McCormick® Ground Black Pepper**
1 can (10 3/4 oz.) cream of mushroom soup
1 cup **Kraft® Shredded Cheddar Cheese**
4 cups frozen **Ore-Ida® Tater Tots®**

directions

1 Preheat oven to 350°F. In a large skillet cook and crumble ground beef until browned. Drain fat. In 2-quart rectangular baking dish layer ground beef. Sprinkle with onion, salt, and pepper.

2 Spread soup over top. Sprinkle with cheese. Arrange potatoes on top. Bake for 40 minutes or until bubbly.

SERVES 6.

Alice George
Wal-Mart #314   Flintville, IN
Alice says this recipe is a favorite with her grandchildren. She likes it because it's so easy to make.

Sausage Veggie Medley

ingredients

1 cup **River®** or **Water Maid® White Rice**

3 medium zucchini, sliced

1 green bell pepper, cut into strips

1 onion, sliced and separated into rings

2 tbsp. olive oil

1 lb. skinless smoked sausage, cut into 1-inch slices

1 1/2 cups fresh cut corn or frozen whole kernel corn

1 can (14 1/2 oz.) **Del Monte® Diced Tomatoes with Basil, Garlic & Oregano**

Salt

McCormick® Ground Black Pepper

1/2 cup **Kraft® 100% Grated Parmesan Cheese**

directions

1 Cook rice according to package directions; set aside. Meanwhile, in 12-inch skillet cook zucchini, bell pepper, and onion in hot oil over medium-high heat about 5 minutes, stirring frequently. Add sausage and corn. Cook and stir 5 minutes more.

2 Add undrained tomatoes. Season to taste with salt and black pepper. Cover and simmer over medium-low heat for 10 minutes or until heated through. Sprinkle with Parmesan cheese. Serve over rice.

SERVES 6.

Craig Brown
Wal-Mart *1812   Wooster, OH
Craig came up with this recipe and both he and his wife loved it. The next day he saw the entry form and decided to enter the contest.

Seafood Salad

ingredients

8 oz. elbow macaroni
1 cup fat-free salad dressing
1 cup fat-free sour cream
2 tbsp milk
1 tbsp. **McCormick® OLD BAY®
Seasoning**
1 tbsp. **McCormick® Garlic Powder**
1 lb. frozen fully-cooked salad shrimp,
thawed
8 oz. imitation crabmeat chunks,
broken up
1 1/2 cups cut-up fresh asparagus
1 medium onion, chopped
Lettuce leaves

directions

1 Cook macaroni according to package directions. Drain. Rinse with cold water. Drain and set aside.

2 In small bowl stir together salad dressing, sour cream, milk, seasoning, and garlic powder. Set aside.

3 In large bowl toss together cooked macaroni, shrimp, imitation crabmeat, asparagus, and onion. Add salad dressing mixture. Toss to coat. Cover and refrigerate for 2 hours. Serve on lettuce-lined plates.

SERVES 10 TO 12.

Lynn Siegel
Wal-Mart #1632 Farwell, MN
*Lynn serves this salad at potluck meals
and family get-togethers.*

Taco Casserole

ingredients

1 lb. lean ground beef

1 pkg. (1.25 oz) **McCormick® Original Taco Seasoning**

1 can (15 1/4 oz.) **Del Monte® Whole Kernel Fiesta® Corn**, drained

1 can (11 oz.) nacho cheese soup

4 cups frozen **Ore-Ida® Tater Tots®** or **Onion Tater Tots®**

directions

1 Preheat oven to 375°F. In large skillet cook beef and taco seasoning according to package directions for taco meat. Transfer meat mixture to 2-quart rectangular baking dish.

2 Spoon corn in an even layer atop meat mixture. Spread soup over corn. Arrange potatoes in a single layer atop the soup.

3 Bake, uncovered, for 40 to 45 minutes or until potatoes are lightly browned and mixture is heated through.

SERVES 6 TO 8.

Carolyn Devers
Wal-Mart *3495   Southside, TN
Carolyn has taken this classic dish to another level by working in taco flavors. She likes to serve the casserole topped with sour cream and salsa.

Taco Salad

Beverly Garza Robertson
Wal-Mart #2010   Niles, MI

During the week when Beverly is pressed for time, she makes the meat mixture the night before and chills it. The next day, all she needs to do is assemble the salad and serve.

ingredients

2 lb. lean ground beef
1 medium onion, chopped
1/2 tsp. each **McCormick® Garlic Powder** and **Ground Cumin**
1 pkg. (1.25 oz.) **McCormick® Original Taco Seasoning**
McCormick® Ground Black Pepper
1 can (15 oz.) **BUSH'S BEST® Black Beans**, rinsed, drained, and chilled
1/2 can (15 1/4 oz.) **Del Monte® Whole Kernel Fiesta® Corn**, chilled*
1 large head iceberg lettuce, chopped
1 pkg. (16 oz.) corn tortilla chips, slightly crushed
1 bottle (16 oz.) Western-style French salad dressing
2 cups **Kraft® Mexican Style Shredded Cheese**
1 ripe avocado, halved, seeded, peeled, and sliced

directions

1 In large skillet cook beef, onion, garlic powder, and cumin until beef is brown; drain fat. Stir in taco seasoning. Season to taste with pepper; cool.

2 To serve, transfer beef mixture to large bowl. Stir in black beans and corn. Add lettuce and chips; toss until combined. Add salad dressing; toss until coated. Top with shredded cheese and avocado.

*Note: Transfer remaining corn to a storage container, cover, and chill for another use.

SERVES 8.

Tangy Barbecued Beef Sandwiches

ingredients

2 1/2-lb. beef chuck roast
2 tbsp. **Enova™ Oil**
2 medium onions, chopped
2 cups ketchup
1 green bell pepper, chopped
2 tbsp. sugar
2 tbsp. yellow mustard
1/2 to 1 tsp. **McCormick® Ground Cinnamon**
1/4 tsp. **McCormick® Ground Cloves**
10 to 12 hamburger buns or kaiser rolls

directions

1 Season roast with salt and pepper. In 4-quart Dutch oven brown roast on all sides in hot oil. Stir in onions and 1/2 cup water. Bring to a boil; reduce heat. Simmer, covered, for 2 to 3 hours or until meat is very tender. Remove roast from Dutch oven. Reserve 1 cup of the cooking liquid; set aside. Discard remaining cooking liquid.

2 In same Dutch oven combine reserved cooking liquid, ketchup, bell pepper, sugar, mustard, cinnamon, and cloves. Bring to a boil; reduce heat. Simmer, covered, for 30 minutes.

3 Meanwhile, use 2 forks to shred meat. Stir shredded meat into ketchup mixture. Simmer, uncovered, for 20 to 30 minutes more until mixture is thickened. Serve in buns.

SERVES 10 TO 12.

Jim Stasky
Wal-Mart #460   Pana, IL
Jim says this family favorite is great for get-togethers instead of hot dogs and burgers. It was originally served as a roast but he decided to try it as a sandwich.

White Chili

ingredients

1 lb. skinless, boneless chicken breast
   halves, diced
1 medium onion, chopped
1 tbsp. **McCormick® Garlic Powder**
2 tbsp. butter
3 cans (16 oz. each.) **BUSH'S® BEST Great
   Northern Beans**, rinsed and drained
1 can (28 oz.) **Del Monte® Diced Tomatoes**
1 jar (16 oz.) mild salsa
4 tsp. **McCormick® Chili Powder**
1 tsp. **McCormick® Ground Cumin**
1/4 cup chopped fresh cilantro
Crushed tortilla chips
Kraft® Shredded Sharp Cheddar Cheese

directions

1 In Dutch oven cook chicken, onion, and
garlic powder in hot butter until chicken is
no longer pink.

2 Stir in beans, undrained tomatoes,
salsa, chili powder, and cumin. Bring to a
boil; reduce heat. Simmer 30 minutes. Stir
in cilantro before serving. Serve with
crushed tortilla chips and shredded
cheese.

SERVES 6 TO 8.

Connie Bailey
Wal-Mart *1233   Royalton, KY
*Connie says that the entire family
loves this easy-to-make recipe
and that leftovers taste just
as good as the first meal.*

Blueberry Muffins

ingredients

1/2 cup milk
1/4 cup **Enova™ Oil**
1 egg
1/2 tsp. **McCormick® Pure Vanilla Extract**
1 1/2 cups all-purpose flour
1/2 cup sugar
2 tsp. baking powder
1/2 tsp. salt
1 cup fresh or 3/4 cup canned blueberries

directions

1 Preheat oven to 400°F. In large bowl beat together milk, oil, egg, and vanilla. Add flour, sugar, baking powder, and salt. Stir just until combined; batter will still be lumpy. Gently fold in blueberries.

2 Spoon into 12 greased muffin cups. Bake for 15 to 20 minutes or until golden brown. Cool in pan.

MAKES 12.

Charlene Rigg
Wal-Mart *5387   Middlefield, OH
Charlene's parents always had blueberries on their property. Making these muffins prompts pleasant memories.

Buttermilk Fruit Salad

ingredients

2 pkg. (4-serving size) **JELL-O® Vanilla Flavor Instant Pudding & Pie Filling**

1 cup buttermilk

1 container (16 oz.) frozen whipped dessert topping, thawed

2 cans (15 1/4 oz. each) **Del Monte® Pineapple Chunks In Its Own Juice**, drained

2 cans (15 1/4 oz. each) **Del Monte® Fruit Cocktail in Syrup**, drained

2 cans (15 oz. each) **Del Monte® Mandarin Oranges**, drained

directions

1 In large bowl stir together pudding mix and buttermilk until well combined. Fold in half the dessert topping. Add pineapple, fruit cocktail, and oranges. Lightly toss until coated.

2 Fold remaining dessert topping into fruit mixture until combined. Cover and chill until serving time.

SERVES 20.

Tammy Wiedbrauk
Wal-Mart #1564   Portsmouth, OH
This make-ahead salad is part of the tradition when Tammy's family gathers for reunions and holidays.

Cheesy Picnic Potatoes

Katie J. Jones
Wal-Mart *1601 Westfield, IN
*Family picnics and other gatherings
aren't complete unless this potato
casserole from Katie's great
aunt is on the menu.*

ingredients

1 pkg. (30 oz.) frozen **Ore-Ida® Country Style Hash Browns**
2 cups **Kraft® Shredded Sharp Cheddar Cheese**
1 carton (16 oz.) sour cream
1 can (10 3/4 oz.) cream of chicken soup
1/2 cup butter, melted
1/4 cup chopped onion
1 tsp. salt
1/4 tsp. **McCormick® Ground Black Pepper**
2 cups cornflakes, crushed
1/4 cup butter, melted

directions

1 Preheat oven to 350°F. In large bowl combine hash browns, cheese, sour cream, soup, 1/2 cup melted butter, onion, salt, and pepper. Spread in 3-quart rectangular baking dish.

2 In small bowl combine cornflakes and 1/4 cup melted butter. Sprinkle over potato mixture.

3 Bake, uncovered, for 45 to 55 minutes or until potatoes are tender.

SERVES 10 TO 12.

Chicken Vegetable Soup with Rotini

ingredients

2 cans (14 oz. each) chicken broth
1 can (14 1/2 oz.) **Del Monte® Cut Green Beans**, drained
1 carrot, thinly sliced
1 rib celery, thinly sliced
1/2 cup sliced mushrooms
1/4 tsp. **McCormick® Ground Thyme**
1/4 tsp. **McCormick® Ground Black Pepper**
3/4 cup rotini pasta
1 pkg. (6 oz.) refrigerated grilled chicken strips, chopped, or 1 cup cubed cooked chicken

directions

1 In large saucepan combine broth, beans, carrot, celery, mushrooms, thyme, and pepper. Bring to a boil. Stir in pasta; reduce heat. Cover and simmer for 10 minutes or until pasta is tender.

2 Stir in chicken. Heat through.

SERVES 4 TO 6.

Jason Kau
Wal-Mart #1459   Indianapolis, IN
This is a quick and easy soup to prepare. It makes a good companion to a grilled cheese sandwich for a light lunch.

Cindy's Famous Baked Beans

Cindy J. Soltis
Wal-Mart #1634   Royalton, MN
*Cindy created this recipe to use
up leftover pineapple. Now it's the
only way she makes baked beans.*

ingredients

4 cans (16 oz. each) **BUSH'S® Original
   Baked Beans**
1 can (20 oz.) **Del Monte® Crushed
   Pineapple In Its Own Juice**, drained
1 cup molasses
1 cup barbecue sauce
2 tbsp. brown or yellow mustard
1 can (6 oz.) French-fried onions
5 slices bacon, crisp-cooked, drained, and
   crumbled
1/8 tsp. **McCormick® Ground Black
   Pepper**

directions

1 Preheat oven to 350°F. In large bowl
stir together beans, pineapple, molasses,
barbecue sauce, and mustard. Stir in
one-third of the onions, one-third of the
bacon, and pepper.

2 Pour into 3-quart rectangular baking
dish. Sprinkle remaining onions and bacon
on top. Bake for 45 to 50 minutes or until
bubbly.

SERVES 12 TO 16.

Cowboy Beans

ingredients

8 oz. bacon, chopped

1 lb. lean ground beef

1/2 cup chopped onion

1 can (28 oz.) **BUSH'S® Barbecue** or **Original Baked Beans**

1 can (16 oz.) **BUSH'S BEST® Large Butter Beans**, rinsed and drained

1 can (16 oz.) **BUSH'S BEST® Dark** or **Light Red Kidney Beans**, rinsed and drained

1 can (15 oz.) **BUSH'S BEST® Black Beans**, rinsed and drained

1/2 to 1 cup packed brown sugar

1/2 to 1 cup hickory-flavored barbecue sauce

2 to 4 tbsp. bottled hot pepper sauce

1 can (14 1/2 oz.) **Del Monte® Cut Green Beans**, drained

directions

1 In large skillet cook bacon until almost crisp; drain on paper towels. In the same skillet cook beef and onion until beef is brown. Drain fat.

2 Transfer beef mixture and bacon to 3 1/2- to 4-quart crockery slow cooker. Gently stir in baked beans, butter beans, kidney beans, black beans, brown sugar, barbecue sauce, and hot sauce. Cover and cook on low-heat setting for 3 to 4 hours.

3 Just before serving, gently stir in green beans. Cover and cook just until green beans are heated through.

SERVES 14 TO 18.

Viola Braun
Wal-Mart *1433   Coldwater, OH
When Viola is asked to bring a dish to a party, she brings this "pot" of beans.

Creamy Cheddar Potatoes

ingredients

1/2 cup butter
2 cups **Kraft® Shredded Cheddar Cheese**
1 carton (16 oz.) sour cream
1/4 cup chopped onion
1/2 to 1 tsp. salt
1 pkg. (30 oz.) frozen **Ore-Ida® Country Style Hash Browns**

directions

1 Preheat oven to 350°F. In large saucepan melt butter over low heat. Stir in cheese. Heat and stir for 2 minutes; remove saucepan from heat. Stir in sour cream, onion, and salt. Stir in hash browns until combined. Spread mixture in a 3-quart rectangular baking dish.

2 Bake, uncovered, for 50 to 55 minutes or until potatoes begin to brown around edges and are tender.

SERVES 10 TO 12.

Barb Lawson
Wal-Mart *1239   Cable, OH
When Barb serves these with ham and green beans, her family says it's "the perfect ending to a long day."

Crisp Oven Potatoes

ingredients

3 cans (2.8 oz. each) French-fried onions, finely crushed

3 tbsp. **Kraft® 100% Grated Parmesan Cheese**

1 tsp. **McCormick® Paprika**

1/2 tsp. **McCormick® Onion Powder**

1/4 tsp. **McCormick® Garlic Powder**

3 large potatoes (2 lb.), peeled and sliced 1/4 inch thick

1/4 cup butter, melted

1/2 to 1 cup **Kraft ® Finely Shredded Cheddar Cheese**

Sour cream (optional)

directions

1 Preheat oven to 375°F. In large resealable plastic bag combine crushed onions, Parmesan cheese, paprika, onion powder, and garlic powder.

2 In large bowl combine potato slices and butter; toss to coat. Using a slotted spoon, transfer potato slices to plastic bag with crumb mixture. Seal bag; shake to coat potato slices. Arrange potato slices on large baking sheet; sprinkle remaining onion mixture over potatoes.

3 Bake for 20 to 25 minutes or until potatoes are tender. Sprinkle potatoes with Cheddar cheese. Bake 1 to 2 minutes more or until cheese is melted. If desired, serve with sour cream.

SERVES 6 TO 8.

Nancy Harter

Wal-Mart *2447   Cincinnati, OH

Nancy combined ideas from several recipes to create this easy side dish. The onions can be crushed with a rolling pin or in a food processor.

Crunchy Ranch Potatoes

Lucas Keeran
Wal-Mart *3765   Saint Paris, OH
Lucas likes to make this recipe with kids because it is simple and delicious. The flavor combination will impress adults as well.

ingredients

3 lb. (about 9 medium) russet potatoes
1 cup bottled ranch salad dressing
1 carton (8 oz.) sour cream
1 cup **Kraft® Shredded Cheddar Cheese**
1/4 cup crisp-cooked, crumbled bacon
1 cup crushed cornflakes
2 tbsp. butter, melted
1/2 tsp. salt

directions

1 Preheat oven to 425°F. Scrub potatoes. Prick potatoes with fork. Place on baking sheet. Bake for 45 to 50 minutes or until tender. Cool potatoes slightly. Reduce oven temperature to 350°F.

2 Meanwhile, in medium bowl stir together salad dressing, sour cream, 1/2 cup of the cheese, and bacon. In small bowl stir together cornflakes and butter. Set aside.

3 Cut potatoes lengthwise into quarters and arrange in 3-quart rectangular baking dish. Sprinkle with salt. Spoon dressing mixture over potatoes. Sprinkle with remaining 1/2 cup cheese. Sprinkle with cornflake mixture. Bake, uncovered, about 20 minutes or until heated through.

SERVES 8 TO 10.

Fabulous Cranberry Salad

Lynnae Nesbit
Wal-Mart *3761 Thief River Falls, MN
Lynnae always freezes cranberries when they're available so she can make this salad in the summer as well as for Thanksgiving and Christmas.

ingredients

1 pkg. (12 oz.) fresh or frozen cranberries
1 can (20 oz.) **Del Monte® Crushed Pineapple In Its Own Juice**, drained
1 cup sugar or **SPLENDA® No Calorie Sweetener, Granular**
1 1/2 tbsp. lemon juice
3/4 pkg. (10.5 oz.) miniature marshmallows
1 container (8 oz.) frozen whipped dessert topping, thawed

directions

1 In blender or food processor blend or process about 1 cup of cranberries until well chopped. Transfer berries to mixing bowl and repeat with remaining cranberries.

2 Add pineapple, sugar, and lemon juice to cranberries. Stir until sugar is dissolved. Add marshmallows and mix thoroughly. Cover and chill for 2 hours.

3 Just before serving, stir in dessert topping.

SERVES 12.

Fruit Salad

ingredients

1 pkg. (16 oz.) frozen sliced strawberries, thawed

1 can (15 1/4 oz.) **Del Monte® Pineapple Tidbits In Its Own Juice**

1 can (15 oz.) **Del Monte® Lite Yellow Cling Sliced Peaches**

1 can (11 oz.) mandarin orange sections

2 ripe bananas, sliced

1 pkg. (4-serving size) **JELL-O® Vanilla Flavor Fat Free Sugar Free Instant Reduced Calorie Pudding & Pie Filling** or **JELL-O® Vanilla Flavor Instant Pudding & Pie Filling**

directions

1 Drain strawberries, pineapple, peaches, and mandarin oranges reserving 1 cup of the juices. In large bowl combine drained fruits and banana.

2 In small bowl combine the 1 cup fruit juice and pudding mix; mix well. Spoon pudding mixture over fruits; toss to mix. Cover and chill for 2 to 4 hours.

SERVES 12.

Chery Mattingly
Wal-Mart #1675   Lebanon, KY
Chery says this salad is "quick, easy, and delicious!"

Grape Salad

ingredients

- 1/2 pkg. (8 oz.) **Philadelphia® Neufchatel Cheese, 1/3 Less Fat than Cream Cheese**, softened
- 1/2 carton (8 oz.) light sour cream
- 1/4 cup **SPLENDA® No Calorie Sweetener, Granular**
- 2 lb. large seedless red grapes
- 2 lb. large seedless green grapes
- 1 tbsp. butter, melted
- 1/4 tsp. **McCormick® Pure Almond Extract**
- 1/2 cup flaked coconut
- 1/2 cup chopped pecans, toasted if desired
- 1/4 cup **SPLENDA® Brown Sugar Blend**

directions

1 In large bowl beat cheese, sour cream, and sweetener with electric mixer until well combined. Fold in grapes.

2 In medium bowl stir together melted butter and almond extract; stir in coconut, pecans, and sweetener. Sprinkle over grape mixture and stir to coat. Cover and chill for 2 to 18 hours.

SERVES 12 TO 16.

Kimberly R. Dojan
Wal-Mart *2421   St. Croix Falls, WI
Kim adapted her mother's make-ahead recipe to use less sugar, but still have the light caramel-like flavor.

Holiday Salad

Cecelia Waller
Wal-Mart *674   Hendersonville, TN

*Cecelia's mother gave her the recipe
for this colorful salad. It's become
a favorite at their Thanksgiving
and Christmas dinners.*

ingredients

1 can (15 oz.) **Del Monte® Lite Fruit Cocktail in Extra Light Syrup**

2 pkg. (8 oz. each) **Philadelphia® Cream Cheese**, softened

1 can (8 oz.) **Del Monte® Crushed Pineapple In Its Own Juice**, drained

1 jar (10 oz.) maraschino cherries, drained and halved

1/2 cup chopped pecans

1 container (8 oz.) frozen whipped dessert topping, thawed

1 pkg. (10.5 oz.) miniature marshmallows

directions

1 Drain fruit cocktail, reserving 4 tablespoons syrup. In medium bowl beat cream cheese and reserved syrup with electric mixer until creamy. Stir in fruit cocktail, pineapple, cherries and pecans. Fold in dessert topping, then fold in marshmallows.

2 Transfer fruit mixture to large serving bowl. Cover and chill for 2 hours before serving.

SERVES 8 TO 12.

Mandarin Orange Salad

ingredients

60 buttery crackers, crushed (about
     2 1/2 cups)
1/2 cup butter, melted
1/4 cup sugar
1 can (14 oz.) sweetened condensed milk
1 can (6 oz.) frozen orange juice
     concentrate, thawed
1 container (8 oz.) frozen whipped
     dessert topping, thawed
3 cans (15 oz. each) **Del Monte® Mandarin
     Oranges**, well drained

directions

1 In medium bowl combine cracker
crumbs, butter, and sugar. Set aside
1/2 cup of crumb mixture for topping.
Press remaining crumb mixture into
bottom of 13x9x2-inch baking dish.
Set aside.

2 In medium bowl combine condensed
milk and orange juice. Fold in dessert
topping and 2 cans of mandarin oranges.
Pour over crust. Sprinkle with reserved
crumb mixture.

3 Garnish with remaining 1 can oranges.
Cover and freeze about 8 hours or until
firm.

SERVES 12 TO 15.

Vicki Smith
Wal-Mart #3262   Cambridge, OH
*In Vicki's household this frosty salad is
both a summer and holiday favorite.*

Mexican Cornbread

ingredients

1 cup self-rising cornmeal mix
1 tbsp. self-rising flour
1 can (14.75-oz.) **Del Monte® Cream Style Golden Sweet Corn**
1/3 cup **Enova™ Oil**
1 egg, lightly beaten
1 medium green bell pepper, chopped
1 medium onion, chopped
1 large jalapeño pepper, seeded and chopped*
1 pkg. (8 oz.) **Kraft® Colby Cheese**, shredded

directions

1 Preheat oven to 350°F. Lightly grease 8- or 9-inch square baking pan; set aside.

2 In medium bowl combine cornmeal mix and flour. Stir in corn, oil, and egg. Stir in bell pepper, onion, and jalapeño pepper. Pour half of the batter into prepared pan. Sprinkle with half of the cheese. Cover with remaining batter and sprinkle with remaining cheese.

3 Bake 45 to 55 minutes or until or a toothpick inserted near center comes out clean and edges are golden brown.

Note: Use caution when handling hot peppers. Wear disposable gloves or wash hands thoroughly after preparation.

SERVES 8.

Laureta Justice
Wal-Mart *2548   Pinsonfork, KY
Laureta has been making this jalapeño- and cheese-flavored cornbread for more than 20 years.

Oven-Baked Potato Pancakes

ingredients

1/3 cup **Enova™ Oil**
5 cups frozen **Ore-Ida® Country Style
    Hash Browns**, thawed
3/4 cup finely chopped onion
2 eggs, beaten
1/2 tsp. salt
1/4 to 1/2 tsp. **McCormick® Ground Black
    Pepper**
Sour cream (optional)

directions

1 Preheat oven to 400°F. Spread oil in 15x10x1-inch baking pan. Place baking pan in oven for 5 minutes to heat oil.

2 In medium bowl combine potatoes, onion, eggs, salt, and pepper.

3 Carefully remove baking pan with hot oil from oven to wire rack. Spoon potato mixture by rounded tablespoons onto pan. Flatten potato mounds with back of spoon. Bake for 15 to 20 minutes or until bottoms begin to brown. Turn pancakes; continue baking about 15 minutes more or until golden brown. Drain on paper towels. Serve with sour cream, if desired.

MAKES 12 (3-INCH) PANCAKES.

Carol L. Fennell
Wal-Mart *2692   Clinton Twp., MI
*Instead of frying potato pancakes,
Carol likes this easy, no-mess
baked version for making them.*

Paul's Banana Nut Muffins

ingredients

1 pkg. (2-layer size) yellow cake mix

1 pkg. (6.4 to 7.6 oz.) banana nut muffin mix

1 pkg. (4-serving size) **JELL-O® Banana Cream Flavor Instant Pudding & Pie Filling**

1 1/3 cups water

3 eggs

2/3 cup **Enova™ Oil**

directions

1 Preheat oven to 350°F. Place paper liners in twenty-six 2 1/2-inch muffin pans or grease muffin pans. Set aside.

2 In large mixing bowl combine cake mix, muffin mix, pudding mix, water, eggs and oil. Beat with an electric mixer on low speed until combined. Beat on medium to high speed about 2 minutes or until batter is smooth.

3 Pour batter into prepared pans. Bake muffins for 20 to 25 minutes or until a wooden toothpick inserted in the center of muffin comes out clean.

MAKES 26 MUFFINS.

Carrie S. Redden
Wal-Mart #477 Soddy-Daisy, TN
Carrie likes to give a basket of these tender muffins for gifts. They're also a good choice for bake sales.

Pineapple Lime Salad

ingredients

1 can (8 oz.) **Del Monte® Crushed Pineapple In Its Own Juice**
1 pkg. (4 serving size) **JELL-O® Brand Lime Flavor Gelatin**
1 cup boiling water
2 pkg. (8 oz.) **Philadelphia® Cream Cheese**, softened and cut into small pieces
1 cup chopped celery (optional)
1/2 cup chopped pecans

directions

1 Drain pineapple, reserving juice; set aside.

2 In medium bowl stir together gelatin and boiling water for 2 minutes or until gelatin is dissolved. Stir in reserved pineapple juice. Stir in cream cheese till blended. If necessary, whisk mixture till cheese is blended.

3 Stir in pineapple, and, if desired, celery until combined. Pour into 2-quart baking dish or serving dish. Sprinkle with pecans. Chill 3 hours or until set.

SERVES 8 TO 10.

Melisa Yerger
Wal-Mart *1330   Lima, OH
Melisa often serves this salad for holiday dinners.

Potato Salad with Hot Bacon Dressing

Judy Chevalier
Wal-Mart *3505   Oxford, WI
*Judy received this popular recipe
from her mother-in-law and also uses
the dressing on dandelion greens,
lettuce, cucumbers, and cabbage.*

ingredients

3 lb. potatoes (about 9 medium), peeled
  and cut into 1-inch pieces
6 slices bacon, cut into small pieces
1 cup sugar or **SPLENDA® No Calorie
  Sweetener, Granular**
2 tbsp. cornstarch
1 to 2 tsp. **McCormick® Ground Mustard**
1/2 tsp. salt
1 1/4 cups water
1/2 cup cider vinegar
4 cups fresh spinach or chopped curly
  endive

directions

1 In 4-quart Dutch oven combine
potatoes and enough water to cover. Bring
to a boil; reduce heat. Cover and simmer
about 10 minutes or until tender. Drain. Set
potatoes aside.

2 In large skillet cook bacon until crisp.
Set aside. In small bowl stir together sugar,
cornstarch, mustard, and salt. Stir in water
and vinegar. Add to bacon and drippings
in skillet. Cook and stir over medium heat
until mixture comes to a boil. Cook and
stir for 2 minutes.

3 Toss together potatoes and greens.
Pour dressing over potato mixture. Toss
to coat. Serve warm.

SERVES 10 TO 12.

Rhubarb Bread

Mabel Wong
Wal-Mart *2198   Minneapolis, MN
If using frozen rhubarb, measure it while frozen and chop any large slices; thaw completely and drain thoroughly before adding to batter.

ingredients

2 1/2 cups flour
1 tsp. baking soda
1/2 tsp. salt
1 1/2 cups packed brown sugar
1 cup buttermilk
2/3 cup **Enova™ Oil**
2 eggs, lightly beaten
1 tsp. **McCormick® Pure Vanilla Extract**
1 1/2 cups chopped fresh rhubarb or
  frozen unsweetened sliced rhubarb
1/2 cup chopped walnuts

directions

1 Preheat oven to 325°F. Grease and flour two 7 1/2x3 1/2x2-inch or 8x4x2-inch loaf pans on bottom and 1/2 inch up sides.

2 In large bowl stir together flour, soda, and salt. Make well in center of dry ingredients. Set aside.

3 In another large bowl stir together brown sugar, buttermilk, oil, eggs, and vanilla. Add sugar mixture to flour mixture, stirring just until combined. Fold in rhubarb and walnuts. Divide batter and pour into pans.

4 Bake for 50 to 60 minutes or until wooden toothpick inserted near centers comes out clean. Cool on wire rack 10 minutes. Run knife around edges of pans to loosen. Remove from pans; cool completely.

MAKES 2 LOAVES (16 SLICES EACH).

Southern Fried Potatoes

ingredients

4 to 6 medium potatoes (about 2 lb.)
2 cups buttermilk self-rising cornmeal mix
1/4 cup self-rising flour
1 tsp. salt
1 tsp. **McCormick® Ground Black Pepper**
1 cup **Enova™ Oil**

directions

1 Peel potatoes and cut lengthwise into 4 or 5 thick slices. Place potatoes in large bowl. Cover with warm water.

2 In resealable plastic bag shake together cornmeal mix, flour, salt, and pepper.

3 In large deep skillet heat oil over medium heat.

4 Drain potatoes and add to flour mixture. Seal bag. Shake until pieces are well coated.

5 Cook potatoes in hot oil over medium-low heat for 5 to 6 minutes or until tender and golden brown, turning once.

SERVES 6.

Missie Johnson
Wal-Mart *3362   Woodlawn, TN
Missie's father prepared these potatoes on Sunday mornings. They are also good with barbecue chicken and biscuits.

Summer Salad Supreme

ingredients

1 can (15 1/4 oz. each) **Del Monte® Whole Kernel Golden Sweet Corn,** drained
1 can (14 1/2 oz. each) **Del Monte® Sauerkraut,** rinsed and drained
1 can (15 oz.) **BUSH'S® BEST Black Beans,** rinsed and drained
1 to 2 tomatoes, chopped
1 medium cucumber, peeled, seeded, and chopped
1 green bell pepper, chopped
6 tbsp. sugar
4 1/2 tbsp. red wine vinegar
4 1/2 tsp. **McCormick® Yellow Mustard Seed**
3/4 tsp. **McCormick® Celery Salt**
Salt
McCormick® Ground Black Pepper

directions

1 In large bowl combine corn, sauerkraut, black beans, tomatoes, cucumber, and bell pepper.

2 In small bowl whisk together sugar, vinegar, mustard seed, and celery salt. Drizzle over corn mixture. Toss to coat. Season to taste with salt and pepper. Cover and chill up to 24 hours.

MAKES 8 TO 10 SERVINGS.

Tomato-Cucumber Salad

ingredients

5 or 6 large ripe tomatoes
2 or 3 medium cucumbers
1 large sweet onion or red onion
1 large green bell pepper
1/2 cup cider vinegar
1/2 cup **Enova™ Oil**
1/4 cup sugar or **SPLENDA® No Calorie Sweetener, Granular**
1 tsp. **McCormick® California Style Crushed Garlic, Wet**
1/2 tsp. salt
1/2 tsp. each **McCormick® Basil Leaves, Oregano Leaves**, and **McCormick® Ground Black Pepper**

directions

1 Coarsely chop tomatoes, cucumbers, onion, and bell pepper. Transfer to large bowl.

2 In small bowl combine vinegar, oil, sugar, garlic, salt, basil, oregano, and pepper. Pour over vegetables. Toss to combine. Cover and chill at least 2 hours before serving.

SERVES 8 TO 10.

Judy Keller
Wal-Mart #233   Cobden, IL
Judy likes to substitute different vegetables, such as yellow or red bell peppers, jalapeño peppers, zucchini, celery, or whatever is ripe in her garden.

Apple Cake

Angi Doble
Wal-Mart #1634   Little Falls, MN
This moist cake is loved by Angi's whole family. The cinnamon smell is especially welcomed when baked in the fall or winter.

ingredients

2 cups all-purpose flour
2 tsp. baking soda
1 tsp. **McCormick® Ground Cinnamon**
3/4 tsp. **McCormick® Ground Nutmeg**
1/2 tsp. salt
1/2 cup butter, softened
2 cups granulated sugar
2 eggs
5 medium cooking apples, peeled and
    finely chopped
2 cups packed brown sugar
1 cup half-and-half or light cream
2/3 cup butter

directions

1 Preheat oven to 350°F. Grease 13x9x2-inch baking pan; set aside. In medium bowl stir together flour, soda, cinnamon, nutmeg, and salt.

2 In large mixing bowl beat the 1/2 cup butter and granulated sugar until fluffy. Add eggs and beat until combined. Beat in flour mixture. Stir in apples. Batter will be stiff.

3 Spread mixture in prepared pan. Bake for 40 to 45 minutes or until toothpick inserted near center comes out clean. Cool slightly in pan on wire rack.

4 Meanwhile, in medium saucepan heat and stir brown sugar, cream, and 2/3 cup butter over medium heat until brown sugar and butter are melted. Spoon warm sauce over servings of warm cake. Refrigerate any remaining sauce.

SERVES 12 TO 16.

Apricot Nectar Cake

Jack Ray Young
Wal-Mart #264   Dickson, TN
*A buttery syrup poured over the
hot cake adds to the moistness
of this light-textured cake.*

ingredients

1 pkg. (2-layer size) vanilla or French
vanilla cake mix
1 pkg. (4-serving size) **Jell-O® French
Vanilla Flavor Instant Pudding & Pie
Filling**
1/2 cup apricot nectar
1/2 cup **Enova™ Oil**
4 eggs
1 cup sugar
1/2 cup butter
Whipped cream (optional)
Dried apricots, thinly sliced (optional)

directions

1 Preheat oven to 350°F. Spray 10-inch
fluted tube pan with nonstick cooking
spray.

2 In mixing bowl combine cake mix,
pudding mix, apricot nectar, oil, 1/2 cup
water, and eggs. Beat on low speed for
30 seconds. Scrape bowl. Beat on
medium speed for 4 minutes. Pour into
prepared pan.

3 Bake for 45 minutes or until a
toothpick inserted in center comes out
clean. Cake will puff up and crack on top
while baking.

4 In saucepan combine sugar, butter, and
1/4 cup water. Heat to a boil, stirring until
sugar is dissolved. Slowly pour over hot
cake in pan, allowing syrup to soak into
cake and drip between cake and edges
of pan. Let stand for 2 minutes then turn
cake out onto cake plate. If desired, serve
cake with whipped cream and garnish with
apricots.

SERVES 12.

Best Pineapple Cake

Sharon Hicks
Wal-Mart *3251   New Holland, OH
*This easy-to-prepare, moist
cake doesn't last long at Sharon's
house. It's a family favorite for special
occasions and for ordinary days.*

ingredients

2 cups all-purpose flour
2 cups granulated sugar
2 tsp. baking soda
1 can (20 oz.) **Del Monte® Crushed
   Pineapple In Its Own Juice**
2 eggs, slightly beaten
2 tsp. **McCormick® Pure Vanilla Extract**
1 cup chopped walnuts (optional)
1 pkg. (8 oz. each) **Philadelphia® Cream
   Cheese**, softened
1/2 cup butter, softened
1 1/2 cups sifted powdered sugar
Chopped walnuts (optional)

directions

1 Preheat oven to 350°F. Grease
13x9x2-inch baking pan; set aside.

2 In large bowl combine flour, sugar, and
baking soda. Stir in undrained crushed
pineapple, eggs, and 1 teaspoon of the
vanilla until just combined (do not
overmix). Stir in 1 cup walnuts, if desired.
Spread batter into prepared pan. Bake
for 30 to 35 minutes or until golden brown
and toothpick inserted in center comes
out clean. Cool in pan on wire rack for
30 minutes.

3 In medium mixing bowl beat cream
cheese, butter, and 1 teaspoon vanilla with
an electric mixer on medium speed until
fluffy. Gradually beat in powdered sugar.
Spread over warm cake. Sprinkle with
additional walnuts, if desired. Cool
completely. Cover and chill.

SERVES 12 TO 15.

Black Walnut Cake

ingredients

2 cups all-purpose flour
1 tsp. baking soda
2 cups granulated sugar
1/2 cup butter
1/2 cup **Enova™ Oil**
5 eggs, separated
1 cup buttermilk
1 tsp. **McCormick® Pure Vanilla Extract**
1 cup shredded coconut
1 cup chopped black walnuts or pecans
Cream Cheese Frosting

directions

1 Preheat oven to 350°F. Grease and lightly flour three 8x1 1/2-inch round baking pans. In small bowl combine flour and soda. Set aside.

2 In large bowl beat granulated sugar, butter, and oil with electric mixer until combined. Beat in egg yolks, buttermilk, and vanilla alternately with flour mixture. Mix in coconut and 1 cup of the nuts.

3 Wash and dry beater. In medium bowl beat egg whites with electric mixer on high speed until stiff peaks form (tips stand straight). Fold egg whites into batter.

4 Pour batter into prepared baking pans. Bake 25 to 30 minutes or until toothpick inserted near center comes out clean. Cool cakes in pans on wire rack for 10 minutes. Remove cakes from pans and cool completely on wire rack.

5 Fill and frost with Cream Cheese Frosting: In medium bowl beat 1 tub (12 ounces) **Philadelphia® Soft Cream Cheese Spread**, 1/2 cup butter, and 2 teaspoons vanilla until smooth. Slowly beat in 3 cups sifted powdered sugar. Then beat in enough of 3 cups powdered sugar to make smooth and spreadable. Stir in 1 cup chopped black walnuts or pecans.

SERVES 16.

Twila Norris
Wal-Mart #687   Crossville, TN
Truly a winning recipe—Twila won first prize at her local fair with this luscious nut-studded cake.

Brownie Fruit Trifle

Brenda Wampler
Wal-Mart #5029   Monroe, MI
*For special occasions, Brenda ties
a pretty ribbon around the bowl
before serving the trifle.*

ingredients

1/2 cup butter
2/3 cup semisweet chocolate pieces
1 cup **SPLENDA® Sugar Blend for Baking**
2 eggs
1 tsp. vanilla
3/4 cup all-purpose flour
1/2 cup chopped walnuts or pecans
   (optional)
3 cups cold milk
2 pkg. (4-serving size) **JELL-O® Sugar-Free Chocolate Flavor Instant Pudding & Pie Filling** or Sugar-Free Vanilla Flavor Instant Pudding & Pie Filling
1 container (8 oz.) frozen whipped dessert topping, thawed
1 lb. fresh strawberries or red raspberries

directions

1 Preheat oven to 350°F. Grease and flour 8x8x2-inch baking pan. Set aside.

2 In medium saucepan cook and stir butter and chocolate over low heat until melted. Remove from heat. Stir in sweetener. Add eggs and vanilla; mix well. Stir in flour and nuts (if desired). Spread in prepared pan.

3 Bake for 25 to 30 minutes. Cool completely on wire rack. Cut into 1x1-inch pieces.

4 Meanwhile, in medium bowl whisk together milk and pudding mix until thick. Fold in half of the dessert topping.

5 In large glass bowl alternately layer pudding mixture, brownie pieces, dessert topping, and fruit. Cover and chill at least 2 hours.

SERVES 10.

Brownie Pizza

ingredients

1/2 cup butter
2 oz. unsweetened chocolate
1 cup sugar
3/4 cup flour
2 eggs
1 tsp. **McCormick® Pure Vanilla Extract**
Peanut Butter Frosting

directions

1 Preheat oven to 350°F.

2 For crust, in saucepan on low heat melt butter, unsweetened chocolate, and sugar, stirring until smooth. Remove from heat and stir in flour. Add eggs and vanilla; beat until smooth.

3 Spread on lightly greased 12-inch pizza pan. Bake for 15 to 20 minutes. Do not overbake. Cool on wire rack.

4 Spread crust with Peanut Butter Frosting: In mixing bowl combine 3 cups sifted powdered sugar, 1/2 cup peanut butter, and 1 teaspoon vanilla. Stir in 4 to 6 tablespoons milk, 1 tablespoon at a time, to make spreadable, and, if desired, 1/4 to 1/2 cup candy-coated chocolate pieces.

SERVES 10.

Linda Helgerson
Wal-Mart #3488   Kansasville, WI
Linda's family first tasted this at their county fair. Her daughters even wanted to learn how to make it.

Butter Pecan Pumpkin Pie

ingredients

1 qt. butter pecan ice cream, softened
1 9-inch deep dish pastry shell, baked
1 cup canned pumpkin
1/2 cup sugar
1/4 tsp. **McCormick® Ground Cinnamon**
1/4 tsp. **McCormick® Ground Ginger**
1/4 tsp. **McCormick® Ground Nutmeg**
1 cup whipping cream, whipped
1/2 cup caramel ice cream topping
Additional whipped cream
Toasted pecans (optional)

directions

1 Spread ice cream into baked pastry shell. Cover and freeze for 2 hours or until firm.

2 In small mixing bowl combine pumpkin, sugar, cinnamon, ginger, and nutmeg. Fold in whipped cream. Spread over ice cream. Cover and freeze for 2 hours or until firm.

3 Remove from freezer 15 minutes before slicing. Drizzle with ice cream topping. Serve with additional whipped cream. If desired, sprinkle with toasted pecans.

SERVES 6 TO 8.

Bonnie Hattery
Wal-Mart *5185   Columbus, OH
Bonnie's refreshing summer or holiday dessert is easy to prepare and can be frozen for up to two months.

Chocolate Almond Cranberry Fudge

ingredients

1 pkg. (11.5 oz.) milk chocolate pieces
1/2 cup powdered sugar
1 pkg. (3 oz.) **Philadelphia® Cream Cheese**, softened
1/4 cup canned chocolate frosting
1/4 tsp. **McCormick® Pure Almond Extract**
1/4 tsp. **McCormick® Pure Orange Extract**
3/4 cup chopped almonds
2/3 cup orange-flavored dried cranberries

directions

1 Line 9x9x2-inch baking pan with foil, allowing foil to extend over edges of pan; set pan aside.

2 In medium saucepan heat chocolate pieces over low heat until melted and smooth; set aside.

3 In medium bowl stir together powdered sugar, cream cheese, frosting, extracts, 1/2 cup of the almonds, and cranberries until combined. Stir in melted chocolate.

4 Spread mixture into prepared pan. Sprinkle with remaining almonds; press lightly. Cover and chill at least 1 hour or until firm. Use foil to lift candy from pan. Remove foil. Cut into pieces.

MAKES ABOUT 48 1-INCH PIECES.

Ron Gardner
Wal-Mart #2238   Grand Haven, MI
Ron's family enjoys this candy year around and especially at Christmas. The almonds can be toasted if you wish.

Chocolate Peanut Butter Pie

Sue Kittinger
Wal-Mart #2080   Marshall, MI
Sue developed this no-bake pie for a potluck with her co-workers. If desired the fillings can be layered and then swirled for a marble appearance.

ingredients

1 pkg. (4-serving size) **JELL-O® Chocolate Fudge Flavor Instant Pudding & Pie Filling**
2 cups cold milk
1 pkg. (8 oz.) **Philadelphia® Cream Cheese**, softened
1 cup creamy peanut butter
3 tbsp. sugar
1 container (8 oz.) frozen whipped dessert topping, thawed
1 (9-oz.) purchased graham cracker pie crust

directions

1 Prepare pudding mix with milk according to package directions.

2 In large bowl beat cream cheese, peanut butter, and sugar with electric mixer until smooth. Beat pudding mixture into peanut butter mixture on low speed just until combined.

3 Fold half of the dessert topping into pudding mixture. Spoon into purchased crust. Cover and chill for 1 hour. Spread remaining dessert topping over pudding mixture. Cover and chill for 8 hours or until set. Garnish with shaved chocolate, if desired

SERVES 6.

Easy Peanut Butter Cookies

Pat Miller
Wal-Mart *1675   Lebanon, KY
Pat makes these sugar- and flour-free cookies for potluck dinners where they're always a hit.

ingredients

1 cup peanut butter
1 cup **SPLENDA® No Calorie Sweetener, Granular**
1 egg
1 tsp. **McCormick® Pure Vanilla Extract**
SPLENDA® No Calorie Sweetener, Granular

directions

1 Preheat oven to 350°F. In medium bowl combine peanut butter and the 1 cup sweetener. Using a fork, beat until combined. Beat in egg and vanilla.

2 Using 2 tablespoons dough for each cookie, shape into balls (dough will be sticky). Place balls on ungreased baking sheet. Moisten the back of a fork and dip it into additional sweetener. Flatten balls with fork tines, making a criss-cross pattern.

3 Bake for 12 to 14 minutes or until bottoms of cookies are golden brown. (Cookies will crumble more easily if undercooked.) Let cookies stand on cookie sheet for 1 minute. Sprinkle cookies with additional sweetener, if desired. Transfer cookies to wire racks to cool.

MAKES 10 COOKIES.

Frosted Banana Bars

ingredients

2 cups flour
1 tsp. baking soda
1/8 tsp. salt
1 cup butter, softened
2 cups granulated sugar
4 medium bananas, mashed (1 1/3 cups)
3 eggs, slightly beaten
1 tsp. **McCormick® Pure Vanilla Extract**
Vanilla Frosting

directions

1 Preheat oven to 350°F. Grease 15x10x1-inch baking pan. In bowl stir together flour, baking soda, and salt; set aside.

2 In large mixing bowl beat 1/2 cup butter with electric mixer for 30 seconds. Add granulated sugar; beat until combined. Add bananas, eggs, and vanilla. Beat until combined. Add flour mixture and beat on low speed just until combined. Pour batter into prepared pan.

3 Bake for 25 to 30 minutes or until toothpick inserted near center comes out clean. Cool in pan on wire rack.

4 Spread with Vanilla Frosting: In mixing bowl beat 1 package (8 ounces) **Philadelphia® Cream Cheese,** softened; 1/2 cup butter; and 2 teaspoons vanilla with electric mixer on medium speed for 2 to 3 minutes. Gradually add 1 package (1 pound) sifted powdered sugar. Beat until smooth. Store in refrigerator.

SERVES 24.

Cori Elsey
Wal-Mart #5064   Richland, MI
*Making these bars reminds Cori
of her grandmother who
made a similar treat.*

Glorified Rice

Fran Larsen
Wal-Mart #965   Tomah, WI
*Fran sometimes varies this recipe
by using flavored whipped dessert
topping and/or colored marshmallows.*

ingredients

1 cup **Riceland® White Rice**
2 cups water
1 tbsp. butter
1/4 tsp. salt
2 cups miniature marshmallows
1 can (15 1/4 oz.) **Del Monte® Crushed
    Pineapple In Its Own Juice**, drained
1 jar (10 oz.) maraschino cherries, drained
    and coarsely chopped
1/4 cup sugar
1 container (8 oz) frozen whipped dessert
    topping, thawed

directions

1 In medium saucepan combine rice,
water, butter, and salt. Bring to a boil;
reduce heat. Simmer, covered, for 18 to
20 minutes or until rice is tender. Cover
and chill 30 minutes in the refrigerator.

2 In large bowl stir together cooled rice,
marshmallows, pineapple, cherries, and
sugar until combined. Fold in dessert
topping. Cover and chill up to 24 hours
before serving.

SERVES 12.

Grandma's Snickerdoodles

Sheri Hughes
Wal-Mart *2417   Alanson, MI
*Sheri's grandmother always had
fresh cookies ready for visitors. This
was one of her favorite recipes
and makes a large batch.*

ingredients

5 1/2 cups all-purpose flour
4 tsp. **McCormick® Cream of Tartar**
2 tsp. baking soda
1 tsp. salt
2 cups shortening
3 cups sugar
4 eggs
1 tsp. **McCormick® Pure Vanilla Extract**
1/3 cup sugar
2 1/2 tsp. **McCormick® Ground Cinnamon**

directions

1 Preheat oven to 375°F. Grease cookie
sheets. In medium bowl combine flour,
cream of tartar, baking soda, and salt;
set aside.

2 In large mixer bowl beat shortening
and 3 cups sugar with electric mixer until
combined. Beat in eggs and vanilla.
Gradually beat in as much of the flour
mixture as you can. Stir in any remaining
flour mixture.

3 In small dish combine 1/3 cup sugar
and cinnamon. Using 2 tablespoons dough
for each cookie, shape into balls and roll
in sugar-cinnamon mixture. Place balls
2 inches apart on prepared cookie sheet.
Bake 11 to 13 minutes or until lightly golden
and cracked on top. Transfer cookies to
wire racks to cool.

MAKES ABOUT 64 COOKIES.

Hint-of-Lemon Cheesecake

ingredients

1 pkg. (2-layer size) yellow cake mix

4 eggs

2 tbsp. **Enova™ Oil**

2 pkg. (8 oz. each) **Philadelphia® Neufchatel Cheese, 1/3 Less Fat than Cream Cheese**, softened

1/4 cup **SPLENDA® No Calorie Sweetener, Granular**

1 1/2 cup low-fat milk

3 tbsp. lemon juice

1 tbsp. **McCormick® Pure Vanilla Extract**

directions

1 Preheat oven to 300°F. Reserve 1 cup of the cake mix.

2 In medium bowl stir together remaining cake mix, 1 egg, and oil until crumbly. Press onto bottom and about 1 inch up sides of ungreased 13x9x2-inch baking pan. Set aside.

3 In large bowl beat cream cheese with an electric mixer until smooth. Beat in reserved cake mix and sweetener until smooth. Gradually beat in milk until smooth. Beat in remaining eggs, lemon juice, and vanilla just until combined. Pour into crust-lined pan.

4 Bake for 40 to 45 minutes or until top appears set when gently shaken. Cool on wire rack for 1 hour. Cover and chill at least 2 hours or overnight before serving.

SERVES 20.

Robin Glesmer

Wal-Mart *5411 Ionia, MI

The quick preparation time makes this family favorite recipe perfect for any occasion.

Lime Cream Dessert

ingredients

1 pkg. (4-serving size) **JELL-O Brand Lime Flavor Gelatin**
1 cup boiling water
1 1/2 cups graham cracker crumbs
1/3 cup sugar
1/2 cup butter, melted
1 pkg. (8 oz.) **Philadelphia® Cream Cheese**, softened
1 pkg. (3 oz.) **Philadelphia® Cream Cheese**, softened
1 cup sugar
1 tsp. **McCormick® Pure Vanilla Extract**
1 container (8 oz.) frozen whipped dessert topping, thawed

directions

1 In small bowl dissolve gelatin in boiling water. Chill about 30 minutes or until partially set.

2 In small bowl stir together graham cracker crumbs and 1/3 cup sugar. Stir in butter. Press onto bottom of 2-quart square baking dish.

3 Meanwhile, in medium mixing bowl beat cream cheese, the 1 cup sugar, and vanilla with electric mixer on medium speed. Gradually add gelatin to cream cheese mixture, beating until combined.

4 Fold in dessert topping. Pour over crust. Cover and chill at least 4 hours or until set.

SERVES 8.

Cindy Lawson
Wal-Mart *3282   Union Furnace, OH
Cindy sometimes uses this filling to make a pie, filling a 9-ounce purchased graham cracker pie shell.

Mexican Fruit Cake

Vicki Gossett
Wal-Mart #1433   Celina, OH
*This crowd-pleasing cake is a
favorite at Thanksgiving when
Vicki's large family gets together.*

ingredients

2 cups all-purpose flour
2 cups granulated sugar
1 can (20 oz.) **Del Monte® Crushed
   Pineapple In Its Own Juice**
2 eggs, slightly beaten
2 tsp. baking soda
2 1/2 cups chopped walnuts
1 pkg. (8 oz.) **Philadelphia® Cream
   Cheese**, softened
1/2 cup butter, softened
1 tsp. **McCormick® Pure Vanilla Extract**
2 cups sifted powdered sugar

directions

1 Preheat oven to 350°F. Grease and flour
13x9x2-inch baking pan; set aside.

2 In large bowl combine flour, sugar,
pineapple, eggs, and baking soda until just
combined (do not overbeat). Stir in 2 cups
of the walnuts. Spread batter in prepared
pan. Bake for 30 to 35 minutes or until
golden and toothpick inserted near center
comes out clean. Cool in pan on wire rack.

3 In medium bowl beat cream cheese,
butter, and vanilla with an electric mixer
on medium speed. Gradually beat in
powdered sugar. Spread over cooled cake.
Sprinkle with remaining 1/2 cup chopped
walnuts. Store up to 24 hours in the
refrigerator.

SERVES 12 TO 15.

Peach Cream Pie

ingredients

1 1/4 cups flour
1/2 tsp. salt
1/4 cup **Enova™ Oil**
2 tbsp. butter-flavored shortening
2 tbsp. water
1 can (21 oz.) peach pie filling
1/2 pkg. (8 oz.) **Philadelphia® Cream Cheese**, softened
2 eggs
1/2 cup milk
1/4 cup **SPLENDA® No Calorie Sweetener, Granular**
Sliced fresh peaches (optional)

directions

1 Preheat oven to 400°F. In medium bowl stir together flour and salt. Set aside.

2 In small bowl beat oil and shortening with electric mixer on low speed until well combined. Add oil mixture and water to flour mixture. Stir with fork just until combined. Form mixture into ball. On lightly floured surface, roll dough into 12-inch circle. Transfer pastry to 9-inch pie plate. Trim pastry to 1/2 inch beyond edge of pie plate. Crimp edge as desired. Spoon pie filling into pastry-lined pie plate. Set aside.

3 In medium bowl beat cream cheese with electric mixer until smooth. Beat in eggs, milk, and sweetener until smooth. Pour over pie filling.

4 Bake for 10 minutes. Reduce oven temperature to 350°F. Bake 35 minutes more or until knife inserted near center comes out clean. Cool completely. Cover and refrigerate any leftovers. If desired, top each serving with sliced peaches.

SERVES 8.

Cindy Lintz
Wal-Mart *2910   Columbiana, OH
Cindy created this refreshing "new, old fashioned dessert" by combining the flavors a friend remembered enjoying in the past.

Peaches-and-Cream Cake

Trina McAlister
Wal-Mart #1341   Mt. Vernon, IN
*This luscious dessert is a favorite of
Trina's grandpa. It's her contribution
to family cookouts.*

ingredients

1 can (29 oz.) **Del Monte® Sliced Peaches
in Heavy Syrup**
1 2-layer package yellow cake mix
(without pudding in mix)
1 pkg. (6-serving size) **JELL-O® Vanilla
Flavor Instant Pudding & Pie Filling**
4 eggs
1 cup **Enova™ Oil**
1 cup water
1 pkg. (8 oz.) **Philadelphia® Cream
Cheese**, softened
1 cup sugar

directions

1 Preheat oven to 350°F. Grease and flour
13x9x2-inch baking pan. Set aside. Drain
peaches, reserving 6 tablespoons of the
syrup. Chop peaches. Set peaches and
reserved syrup aside.

2 In large bowl beat cake mix, pudding
mix, eggs, oil, and water with electric mixer
until well combined. Pour batter into
prepared pan. Top with chopped peaches.

3 In medium bowl beat cream cheese,
sugar, and reserved peach juice with
electric mixer until smooth. Pour cream
cheese mixture over peaches and cake
batter. Bake for 50 to 55 minutes or until
set in center. Cool completely on wire
rack. Chill 2 hours before cutting. Store
in refrigerator.

SERVES 15.

Peanut Butter Cookies

ingredients

2 cups peanut butter
1 cup butter-flavored shortening
1 cup granulated sugar
1 cup packed brown sugar
1 1/2 tsp. baking soda
1/2 tsp. salt
2 eggs
1 tsp. **McCormick® Pure Vanilla Extract**
3 cups all-purpose flour
Granulated sugar

directions

1 Preheat oven to 375°F. In large bowl stir together peanut butter and shortening with a wooden spoon. Add sugars, baking soda, and salt. Stir until well combined.

2 Add eggs and vanilla. Stir until well combined. Stir in flour until combined.

3 Shape dough into 1-inch balls. Arrange 2 inches apart on ungreased cookie sheets. Use the tines of a fork dipped in sugar to flatten the balls and make a criss-cross pattern.

4 Bake for 8 to 10 minutes or until lightly browned around edges. Let cool on cookie sheets for 1 minute. Remove and cool completely on wire racks. Drizzle with melted chocolate, if desired.

MAKES ABOUT 80 COOKIES.

Donna Preston
Wal-Mart #1752   Bay City, MI
This was one of Donna's aunt's favorite cookie recipes. Donna believes they taste better when mixed with a spoon instead of an electric mixer.

Pineapple Cream Cheese Pie

Joreen Burris
Wal-Mart #1761 Granite City, IL
For Joreen, Easter is a time for celebration and for serving this easy, delicious pie. The filling recipe came from her mother.

ingredients

1 unbaked refrigerated 9-inch piecrust
(1/2 of 15-oz. package)
1 can (8 oz.) **Del Monte® Crushed Pineapple In Its Own Juice**
1/3 cup sugar
1 tbsp. cornstarch
1 pkg. (8 oz.) **Philadelphia® Cream Cheese**, softened
1/2 cup sugar
1/2 cup milk
2 eggs
1/2 tsp. **McCormick® Pure Vanilla Extract**

directions

1 Line 9-inch pie plate with pastry according to package directions.

2 Preheat oven to 400°F. In medium saucepan combine undrained pineapple, 1/3 cup sugar, and cornstarch. Cook and stir over medium heat until mixture comes to a boil. Reduce heat; cook and stir for 2 minutes more or until thickened. Remove from heat. Cool for 10 minutes. Spread pineapple mixture in bottom of piecrust.

3 In medium bowl beat cream cheese, 1/2 cup sugar, milk, eggs, and vanilla with electric mixer until smooth. Pour cream cheese mixture evenly over pineapple mixture.

4 Bake for 10 minutes. Reduce oven temperature to 325°F and bake about 35 minutes more or until center is set. Cool completely on wire rack. Cover and store in refrigerator.

SERVES 8.

Pineapple Pecan Pie

ingredients

1 pkg. (8 oz.) **Philadelphia® Cream Cheese**, softened

1 pkg. (1 lb.) powdered sugar

1 can (20 oz.) **Del Monte® Crushed Pineapple In Its Own Juice**, well drained

1 cup chopped pecans

1 container (12 oz.) frozen whipped dessert topping, thawed

2 (9-inch) purchased graham cracker crumb pie shells

directions

1 In large mixing bowl beat cream cheese and sugar with an electric mixer on medium speed until combined.

2 Stir in pineapple and pecans. Fold in dessert topping. Spoon mixture into pie shells.

3 Cover and chill at least 2 hours. (If desired, freeze pie until firm; let frozen pie stand at room temperature about 45 minutes before slicing.)

SERVES 12.

Beverly Robson
Wal-Mart #922   Corydon, IN
Beverly also calls this "Millionaire Pie."
Whether chilled or frozen, it's a hit.

Scalloped Pineapple

ingredients

1 cup butter, softened

2 cups sugar or 1 cup **SPLENDA® Sugar Blend for Baking**

4 eggs, beaten

1/4 cup milk

4 cups cubed white bread

1 can (20 oz.) **Del Monte® Crushed Pineapple In Its Own Juice**

directions

1 Preheat oven to 375°F. Lightly butter a 2-quart rectangular baking dish; set aside.

2 In large mixing bowl beat butter, sugar, and eggs with an electric mixer until creamy. Stir in milk, bread cubes, and undrained pineapple. Pour into prepared dish. (Mixture may look curdled.) Bake 15 minutes. Reduce oven temperature to 350°F. Bake 40 to 50 minutes longer or until top is golden brown.

SERVES 8 TO 10.

Caren Sleyster

Wal-Mart #792   Aledo, IL

Caren likes to serve this easy-to-make and rich-tasting dessert warm with whipped cream.

Sour Cream Raisin Pie

Sally Freeman
Wal-Mart #1750   Marion, OH
*Sally's mother often made
this pie during the holidays.
Raisin lovers always enjoy it.*

ingredients

2 eggs, slightly beaten
3/4 cup sugar
1 tsp. **McCormick® Ground Cinnamon**
1/2 tsp. **McCormick® Ground Nutmeg**
1 carton (8 oz.) sour cream
1/2 cup raisins
1 tsp. finely shredded lemon peel
1/8 tsp. salt
1 9-inch unbaked frozen pie shell

directions

1 Preheat oven to 450°F. In mixing bowl
combine eggs, sugar, cinnamon, and
nutmeg. Stir in sour cream, raisins, lemon
peel, and salt. Pour filling into pie shell.

2 Bake for 10 minutes. Reduce oven
temperature to 325°F and bake about
30 minutes more or until a knife inserted
near the center comes out clean. Cover
and chill to store.

SERVES 8.

Southern Coconut Cake

Barbara Novotny
Wal-Mart *161   Huntingdon, TN
*Barbara calls this recipe
"Southern" because in the
South "We love our cakes
moist and this one is!"*

ingredients

2 cups self-rising flour
2 cups granulated sugar
1 cup **Enova™ Oil**
4 eggs
2 cups milk
1 tbsp. **McCormick® Pure Vanilla Extract**
3/4 cup sweetened flaked coconut
1/4 cup granulated sugar

directions

1 Preheat oven to 350°F. Lightly coat bottom and sides of 13x9x2-inch baking pan with nonstick cooking spray; set aside.

2 In large mixing bowl stir together flour and 2 cups granulated sugar. Add oil, eggs, 1 cup of the milk, and vanilla. Beat with electric mixer on medium speed for 2 minutes. Pour into prepared pan. Bake about 30 minutes or until toothpick inserted near center comes out clean.

3 Meanwhile, in small saucepan heat remaining 1 cup milk, coconut, and 1/4 cup granulated sugar to a boil; reduce heat and simmer 1 minute. Remove from heat.

4 Remove cake from oven. Prick top of hot cake with fork. Pour hot coconut mixture evenly over cake. Cool completely.

5 Prepare icing: In bowl combine 1 1/2 cups sour cream, 1 1/2 cups powdered sugar, and 1 container (8 oz.) frozen whipped dessert topping, thawed. Stir with a spoon until combined. Spread over cooled cake. Sprinkle 1/4 cup coconut over top. Cover and chill.

SERVES 15 TO 20.

Sweet Potato Layer Cake

Joyce Hill
Wal-Mart #253   Jerseyville, IL
*Everyone tells Joyce that her grandmother
was a good cook. This is one of her
passed-down recipes.*

ingredients

2 cups flour
1 tbsp. baking soda
2 tsp. **McCormick® Ground Cinnamon**
1 tsp. salt
1 1/2 cups **Enova™ Oil**
1 cup **SPLENDA® Sugar Blend for Baking**
4 eggs, slightly beaten
1 1/2 cups canned sweet potatoes in syrup,
   drained and mashed
1 cup chopped walnuts
1 tbsp. **McCormick® Pure Vanilla Extract**
1 can (20 oz.) **Del Monte® Crushed Pineapple In
   Its Own Juice**
1/2 cup **SPLENDA® Sugar Blend for Baking**
7 1/2 tsp. cornstarch
Purchased cream cheese frosting

directions

1 Preheat oven to 350°F. Grease and flour three
9x1-inch round baking pans; set aside. Stir together
flour, baking soda, cinnamon, and salt.

2 In large mixing bowl combine oil and 1 cup
sweetener. Beat with electric mixer on medium
speed until combined. Add eggs, 1 at a time,
beating well. Add flour mixture; beat on low
speed just until combined. Stir in mashed sweet
potatoes, walnuts, and 1 tablespoon vanilla. Pour
batter into prepared pans.

3 Bake for 25 to 30 minutes or until toothpick
inserted near center comes out clean. Cool
10 minutes; remove from pans.

4 For filling, in saucepan combine pineapple,
1/2 cup sweetener, and cornstarch. Cook and stir
over medium heat until mixture is thickened. Cool.
Fill cake with pineapple filling. Frost with cream
cheese frosting. Store in refrigerator.

SERVES 12 TO 16.

Bertolli Bruschetta

Prep Time: 10 Minutes
Cook Time: 5 Minutes

ingredients

2 loaves Italian or French bread, diagonally
    cut into 3/4-inch slices
2 large cloves garlic
1/3 cup **Bertolli® Extra Virgin Olive Oil**
1 jar (24 oz.) **Bertolli® Tomato & Basil Sauce**
Bruschetta Toppings

directions

In preheated oven, broil bread slices until
golden; rub with garlic, then brush with olive oil.
Evenly spoon unheated sauce over bread, then
top with your favorite Bruschetta Toppings and
enjoy!

*Here are a few suggestions for Bruschetta Toppings,
or create your own!* Sliced fresh mozzarella with
chopped fresh basil. Sliced fresh mozzarella with
prosciutto and fresh basil. Sliced cooked chicken
and feta cheese, olives, and fresh thyme. Sliced
fresh mozzarella with sliced or chopped roasted
red peppers or sun-dried tomatoes and chopped
fresh basil.

MAKES 24 SERVINGS.

Nutrition Information per serving with mozzarella cheese
and basil: Calories 180, Calories From Fat 80, Saturated
Fat 3g, Trans Fat 0g, Total Fat 9g, Cholesterol 15mg,
Sodium 410mg, Total Carbohydrate 18g, Sugars 3g, Dietary
Fiber 2g, Protein 7g, Vitamin A 6%, Vitamin C 2%, Calcium
15%, Iron 6%.

*Today, over 135 years since
Francesco Bertolli began selling
his olive oil in Lucca, Italy, Bertolli
is still the world's most-loved olive
oil, and is at the heart of authentic Italian cooking.
Bertolli oils and sauces are restaurant inspired flavors
made with only the finest quality ingredients. Savor life
the way Italians do, with simple meals, great times,
quality ingredients, and most of all a passion for life
and cooking.*

Red Beans and Rice

ingredients

1 green bell pepper, chopped
1 medium onion, chopped
3 cloves garlic, chopped
3 ribs celery, chopped
3 tbsp. vegetable oil
1 lb. andouille sausage, sliced (or use any smoked sausage)
2 cans (16 oz.) **BUSH'S® BEST Red Beans**
3 tbsp. Creole seasoning
Hot cooked rice

directions

1 Sauté bell pepper, onion, garlic, and celery in vegetable oil until tender. Add sausage and cook until done. Pour in **BUSH'S® BEST Red Beans** and Creole seasoning. Cook until simmering. Serve over hot cooked rice.

SERVES 6.

Founded in 1908, Bush Brothers & Company is based in Knoxville, Tenn. In addition to the famous baked beans and its lovable commercials featuring Jay Bush and his talking dog Duke, it offers Homestyle Chili and more than 20 varieties of other beans including kidney, pinto, and black. Today, Bush Brothers & Company is still family owned and operated, working for the same ideals that were set forth by A.J. Bush nearly 100 years ago — ensuring the highest quality and best taste can be found in all their products. For more information and other great recipes, visit www.bushbeans.com.

Tuna Corn Quesadilla with Spinach Salad

ingredients

4 (7- to 8-inch) flour tortillas
1 cup shredded pepper Jack cheese
1 STARKIST FLAVOR FRESH POUCH® Tuna, Albacore (7 oz.)
1 cup drained **DEL MONTE® Whole Kernel Yellow Corn**
1 tbsp. chopped cilantro
1 can **DEL MONTE® Diced Tomatoes**
3 cups washed baby spinach leaves
1 can **DEL MONTE® Sliced Peaches in Lite Syrup**, peaches cut in half, juice reserved
1/2 cup chopped red onion
2 tbsp. canola oil
2 tbsp. white wine vinegar

directions

1 Heat a 10-inch nonstick skillet over medium heat. Place 1 tortilla in skillet and cook until starting to brown; turn.

2 Fill 1 side of the tortilla with 1/4 cup cheese, 1/4 cup tuna, 1/4 cup corn, 1/4 cup tomatoes, and one-fourth of the cilantro. Fold other half of the tortilla over mixture. Continue cooking until golden brown and cheese is melted. Repeat for each tortilla.

3 Meanwhile, combine spinach, peaches, and red onion in a bowl. Combine oil, vinegar, and reserved syrup. Toss dressing with the salad.

SERVES 4.

The Del Monte Difference *The Del Monte name goes back more than 100 years and today consumers know the Del Monte brand stands for premium quality, just as it did 100 years ago. Del Monte makes it easy and convenient for your family to get its USDA daily recommendation of fruits and vegetables. Our recipes are kitchen tested with the busy consumer in mind. For more delicious and quick recipes, visit www.delmontedaily.com*

Fruit Bread

ingredients

2 cups all-purpose flour
3/4 cup sugar
3 tsp. baking powder
3/4 tsp. salt
1/4 cup candied pineapple, diced
1/2 cup raisins or currants
1/2 cup candied cherries, chopped
2 eggs
1 cup milk
1/4 cup **Enova™ Oil**

directions

1 Preheat oven to 350°F (175°C). Grease one 9x5x3-inch loaf pan.

2 In a large bowl combine flour, sugar, baking powder, salt, candied pineapple, raisins or currants, and cherries. Stir thoroughly. Make a well in center.

3 In small bowl beat eggs until frothy. Mix in milk and **Enova™ Oil**. Pour into well. Stir just to moisten. Pour into greased 9x5x3-inch loaf pan.

4 Bake at 350°F (175°C) for 1 hour. Let cool in pan 10 minutes, then remove.

MAKES 12 SERVINGS.

Calories 220; Fat 6 g (sat 1g, mono 2.5g, poly 3g); Protein 4g; Cholesterol 35mg; Sodium 280mg; Fiber 1g; Carbohydrate 37g.

Enova Brand Oil is a unique cooking and salad oil with the following benefit: Less is stored in the body as fat. There are two structures found in cooking and salad oils: Triglyceride (TAG) and Diglyceride (DAG). Both are digested and absorbed in the same way, but a majority of DAG is metabolized differently from TAG: less DAG is stored in the body as fat. Most cooking oils, including canola and olive oil, are primarily TAG, with small percentages of DAG. But Enova™ contains at least 80% DAG, the only DAG rich oil available in the market.

Holiday Mix & Match Pudding Pie

ingredients

Take 2 cups cold milk, 2 pkg. (4-serving size each) or 1 pkg. (8-serving size) JELL-O Chocolate or Vanilla Flavor Instant Pudding & Pie Filling and 1 tub (8 oz.) thawed COOL WHIP Whipped Topping and mix & match your recipe from these options...

Recipe Option: Peppermint-Chocolate Pudding Pie
Crust and Filling Choices: HONEY MAID Graham Pie Crust, 1 cup JET-PUFFED Miniature Marshmallows.
Special Extras: 10 peppermint candies, coarsely chopped; wedges of Peppermint Bark.*

Recipe Option: Raspberry Double-Chocolate Pudding Pie
Crust and Filling Choices: OREO Pie Crust, 1 cup fresh raspberries.
Special Extras: 20 fresh raspberries; White Chocolate Curls*; 2 tsp. powdered sugar.

Recipe Option: Black Forest Pudding Pie
Crust and Filling Choices: OREO Pie Crust; 10 OREO Chocolate Sandwich Cookies, quartered.
Special Extras: 1 cup cherry pie filling, drizzle with 1 square melted BAKER'S Semi-Sweet Baking Chocolate.

Recipe Option: Banana Caramel Chocolate Pudding Pie
Crust and Filling Choices: OREO Pie Crust, 1 cup sliced bananas
Special Extras: 13 PLANTERS Pecan Halves, chocolate-dipped*; 5 KRAFT Caramels melted with 1 tsp. milk

More than 100 years ago JELL-O® was little more than a brand name and an unfulfilled dream. Today, America's Most Famous Dessert™ sells more than 640 million JELL-O® products a year. What began in LeRoy, New York, in 1897 as a simple gelatin dessert has changed and adapted with consumers over the past century, and become an American icon with a brand name recognized by 99 percent of Americans. Originally, there were just four flavors of gelatin and now there are more than 158 JELL-O® brand desserts and snacks available.

directions

1 Pour milk into medium bowl. Add dry pudding mixes. Beat with wire whisk 2 minutes or until well blended. (Mixture will be thick.)

2 Spoon 1 1/2 cups of the pudding into 1 (6-oz.) crust; top with filling. Gently stir 1 1/2 cups of the whipped topping into remaining pudding; spoon over pie.

3 Refrigerate 3 hours. Cover with remaining 1 1/2 cups whipped topping just before serving. Top with special extras. Store leftover pie in refrigerator.

*Special Extras

Peppermint Bark: Microwave 4 squares BAKER'S Semi-Sweet Baking Chocolate in microwaveable bowl on HIGH 1 1/2 to 2 minutes or until melted, stirring every 30 seconds. Stir in 1/4 cup crushed peppermint candies (about 10 candies). Spread thinly onto wax paper-covered baking sheet; refrigerate until firm. Break into pieces; place on top of pie.

White Chocolate Curls: Microwave 1 square BAKER'S Premium White Baking Chocolate on HIGH 15 seconds. Slowly pull a vegetable peeler along 1 side of the chocolate square to create a curl. Use wooden pick to arrange curls in center of pie.

Chocolate-Dipped Pecans: Microwave 1 square BAKER'S Semi-Sweet Baking Chocolate in microwaveable bowl on HIGH 30 seconds or until melted; stir. Dip 1 end of each pecan half in chocolate. Place on wax paper-covered baking sheet; refrigerate until firm. Arrange over pie.

MAKES 10 SERVINGS, ONE SLICE EACH.

Holiday Cheese Truffles

Prep: 15 min.
Total: 4 hours 15 min. (incl. refrigerating)

ingredients

2 pkg. (8 oz. each) **PHILADELPHIA Cream Cheese,**
    softened
1 pkg. (8 oz.) **KRAFT Shredded Sharp Cheddar Cheese**
1 tsp. garlic powder
Dash ground red pepper
1/4 cup chopped roasted red peppers
1/4 cup chopped green onions
1 2/3 cups PLANTERS Chopped Pecans
SOCIABLES Savory Crackers

directions

1 Beat cream cheese, shredded cheese, garlic powder, and ground red pepper until well blended. Divide in half. Add roasted red peppers to 1 half and green onions to the other half; mix each half until well blended. Cover.

2 Refrigerate several hours or until chilled.

3 Shape each cheese mixture into 24 balls, each about 1 inch in diameter. Roll in pecans. Cover and refrigerate until ready to serve.

MAKES 24 SERVINGS, 2 TRUFFLES AND 5 CRACKERS EACH.

Size-Wise: Enjoy a single serving of this indulgent holiday treat.

Jazz It Up: Try these other coatings for these tasty truffles — sesame seeds, chopped fresh parsley, paprika and KRAFT Shredded Cheese.

Festive Wreath: Alternately arrange different flavored truffles in a large circle on platter to resemble a holiday wreath. Create a decorative bow out of green onion strips. Use to garnish wreath.

Cheese Logs: Roll each half into a 6-inch log. Roll in desired coatings as directed.

Nutrition Information Per Serving: 230 calories, 19g total fat, 7g saturated fat, 30mg cholesterol, 290mg sodium, 11g carbohydrate, 2g dietary fiber, 2g sugars, 5g protein, 10%DV vitamin A, 4%DV vitamin C, 10%DV calcium, 4%DV iron.

KRAFT®

Americans have a love affair with cheese, and cheese lovers know only one way to spell cheese: K-R-A-F-T. For more than 100 years, this love of cheese has helped make Kraft Cheese an American icon from coast to coast. For over a century, Kraft Cheese has helped families create fond memories, putting satisfied smiles on countless faces and making Mom the real star of the kitchen table.

Vanilla Rich Chip Cake

ingredients

1 pkg. (18 1/4 oz.) yellow cake mix
1 pkg. (3 1/2 oz.) instant vanilla pudding mix
1 cup sour cream
1/2 cup <u>each</u> vegetable oil <u>and</u> water
4 eggs
1 tbsp. **McCormick® Pure Vanilla Extract**
1 cup mini chocolate chips
Vanilla Butter Glaze (recipe follows)

directions

1 Beat all ingredients, except chips, in large bowl with mixer on low speed just to moisten. Beat on medium speed 2 minutes.

2 Stir in chips. Pour into greased and floured 12-cup Bundt pan.

3 Bake in 350°F oven 50 minutes or until toothpick inserted in center comes out clean. Cool in pan 10 minutes. Invert cake onto wire rack. Cool completely. Drizzle with Vanilla Butter Glaze or sprinkle with confectioners' sugar, if desired.

MAKES 16 SERVINGS.

Vanilla Butter Glaze: Mix 3 tbsp. butter, melted, 2 1/4 cups confectioners' sugar, 3 tbsp. water and 1 1/2 tsp. **McCormick® Pure Vanilla Extract** until smooth. Let stand 3 minutes or until thickened.

McCormick & Co. Inc. was founded in 1889 by 25-year-old Willoughby McCormick in Baltimore, Maryland. With his staff of three, the company began producing and selling root beer, flavoring extracts and fruit syrups, and juices door to door. Since the company's beginnings, McCormick has spent more than 100 years pioneering the art of processing and blending the finest natural raw materials into unique food seasonings and flavors. A team of spice buyers explores all parts of the world to find the best spices and herbs available.

McCormick.com is your home for recipes, cooking tips, meal ideas, and in-depth information on the wide range of McCormick products. By registering for My McCormick, you can save your favorite McCormick recipes and articles and receive recipe suggestions based on your preferences. Our test kitchen experts offer handy cooking references and great tips on food preparation. www.mccormick.com

Creamy Brunch Potato Bake

ingredients

2 tbsp. butter or margarine
4 cups **Ore-Ida® Potatoes O'Brien**, thawed
1 clove garlic, minced
1/2 cup chopped onions
1 cup light or regular sour cream
2 eggs, beaten
1/2 tsp. salt
1/2 cup Cheddar cheese
Chopped chives or parsley (optional)

directions

1 Preheat oven to 375°F. Melt butter in a large nonstick skillet over medium heat. Add potatoes, onions, and garlic; cook 8 to 10 minutes or until potatoes are tender, stirring occasionally. Remove from heat; stir in sour cream, eggs, and salt; mix well. Transfer to an ungreased 1 1/2-quart round soufflé or casserole dish. Bake, uncovered, 25 minutes or until set. Top with cheese; continue baking 2 minutes more or until cheese is melted. Sprinkle with chives or parsley, if desired.

SERVES 6.

The Ore-Ida Story. Ore-Ida Potato Products, Inc. was formed in 1952 with its first and largest Ore-Ida® potato-processing facility located in Oregon, right near the border of Idaho. Thus, the brand name "Ore-Ida®" was born, combining the first few letters of Oregon and Idaho. Today, the Ore-Ida® Brand is the most trusted and popular name in the potato and onion business and the nation's leading marketer of frozen potatoes. Visit www.ore-ida.com for more recipes and fun facts from America's favorite potato company.

Brown Rice Recipe Creations

Create your own tasty, satisfying, and nutritious meal, just ...

Prepare 1 cup of **Mahatma®**, **Carolina®**, **River®**, or **Riceland® Brown Rice** or 2 bags (3.5 oz. each) **Success® Boil-In-Bag Brown Rice** according to package directions.

Create an *Italian Medley* (pictured) by combining cooked asparagus tips, toasted pine nuts, and red and yellow peppers with hot cooked brown rice. Top with Parmesan cheese.

Try something green – *Cilantro Cheese Brown Rice*. Just top hot cooked brown rice with diced tomatoes, green onions, Monterey Jack cheese, and cilantro. Sprinkle with Parmesan cheese.

Or, start the day with a *Healthy Breakfast Brown Rice*. Add cooked brown rice to your favorite fruited yogurt. Top with granola and fresh fruit.

Nothing adds more to a healthy meal than fresh ingredients and the natural whole-grain goodness of brown rice. Whether you use Mahatma, Carolina, River, or Riceland Brown Rice, or 10-minute Success Boil-In-Bag Brown Rice you can create a healthy meal for your family. Visit successrice.com, riceland.com, riverrice.com, carolinarice.com, or mahatmarice.com for FREE recipes!!

Gingerbread Cake

Preparation Time: 20 minutes
Baking Time: 50 to 60 minutes

ingredients

2 cups unsweetened applesauce
3/4 cup molasses
1/3 cup vegetable oil
3 eggs
3 cups all-purpose flour
1 1/3 cups **SPLENDA® No Calorie Sweetener, Granular**
2 tsp. baking soda
1 tsp. baking powder
1/2 tsp. salt
2 tsp. ground ginger
1 1/2 tsp. cinnamon
1/2 tsp. ground clove

directions

1 Preheat oven to 350°F. Spray Bundt pan with butter-flavored cooking spray. Set aside.

2 Pour applesauce, molasses, and vegetable oil into a large mixing bowl. Add eggs. Stir well.

3 Blend remaining dry ingredients in a separate bowl. Mix well.

4 Add dry ingredients to the applesauce mixture. Stir well.

5 Pour cake batter into prepared pan. Bake in preheated 350°F oven 50 to 60 minutes, or until a toothpick inserted in the center comes out clean. Remove from oven. Cool cake in pan on a wire rack approximately 20 minutes. Invert cake onto serving plate. Serve warm or cool.

MAKES 18 SERVINGS.

Serving Suggestions Place 1/2 cup **Splenda® Granular** in a blender. Blend, covered, on high approximately 30 seconds. Sprinkle the finely ground Splenda over the cake like powdered sugar. Serve with sautéed apples or non-dairy topping.

Nutrition Information per serving. Serving Size: 1 slice. Total Calories 180; Calories from Fat 45; Total Fat 5g; Saturated Fat 0.5g; Cholesterol 35mg; Sodium 250mg; Total Carbohydrate 31g; Dietary Fiber 1g; Sugars 11g; Protein 3g.

This recipe, when compared to a traditional recipe, has a 45% reduction in calories, a 62% reduction in fat, a 37% reduction in carbohydrates, and a 63% reduction in sugar!

Splenda No Calorie Sweetener

Life is sweet - and SPLENDA® Products make it even sweeter, by giving you a healthy, delicious alternative to sugar. When you replace sugar with SPLENDA® Products, you can eat, drink, and enjoy your favorite recipes with fewer calories and carbohydrates. SPLENDA® No Calorie Sweetener is available in granular form in a 9.7 oz. Baker's Bag, equivalent in sweetness to 5 lb. of sugar, which is ideal for cooking and baking, as well as in 1- and 2-lb. equivalent sweetness boxes and in packet form, too.

The Secrets of Accurate Measuring

Accurate measuring is one of the keys to good cooking. Sometimes, too much or too little of a key ingredient can affect the taste or performance of a recipe.

Dry ingredients should always be measured using plastic or metal measuring cups, which are usually sold in sets of graduated cups ranging from 1 cup to 1/4 or 1/8 cup.

To measure soft or sticky ingredients, such as molasses or peanut butter, try lightly spraying the measuring cup with nonstick cooking spray, so the ingredient will drop out easily.

Liquid ingredients should always be measured in a clear glass or plastic cup. To ensure an accurate measurement, place the measuring cup on a flat surface and read the measurement from eye level.

Measuring spoons, which generally come in sets ranging from 1 tablespoon to 1/4 or 1/8 teaspoon, can be used for dry and liquid ingredients. When measuring dry ingredients such as baking soda or powder, run the straight back of a knife blade across the filled spoon to remove the excess.

Portion Control in the palm of your hand

Not sure how much food is in a single portion? You can determine individual servings by envisioning the average woman's hand.

A 3-ounce serving of meat, poultry or fish is about the size of *the palm of a woman's hand.*

A 1/2-cup serving of pasta, rice, potatoes, fruit or vegetables is about the size of *a woman's tightly-clenched fist.*

A 1-cup serving of cereal, yogurt or greens can fit into *the loosely cupped palm of a woman's hand.*

A 1-ounce serving of hard cheese or chocolate is about the size of *a woman's thumb.*

COMPLIMENTARY
COOKING MAGAZINE OFFER

YOUR OPINION MATTERS!

Please take a moment to respond to our survey. For your response, we will send you a **COMPLIMENTARY** copy of the current issue of "HOMEMADE" magazine! Thank you for participating!

1. What prompted you to purchase the 2007 Wal-Mart Family Cookbook? (Please circle one response)

Appetizing photos   Recipes looked easy to prepare   It was reasonably priced   I'm an avid cook

Purchased previous issues   Looking for new meal ideas   I know someone published in the cookbook

2. Did you purchase any of the brands featured in this book? ☐ Yes ☐ No

If yes, please list purchased items(s)? _____

If no, do you plan to make a purchase of any of the items featured in this cookbook? ☐Yes ☐No

3. What other cookbooks or food themed magazines would you like to find at Wal-Mart? _____

_____

4. Would you attend a Wal-Mart sponsored cooking workshop if it was offered in your area? ☐Yes ☐No

Please provide the following:

Name _____

Address _____

City _____

State/Province _____ Zip/Postal Code _____

Email _____

Please circle your age: 18-24   25-34   35-54   55+

> **WAL-MART WOULD LOVE TO HEAR FROM YOU, AND WE WANT YOUR ORIGINAL RECIPES!**
> If you are interested in submitting your own recipe for a chance to be published in the new Wal-Mart cooking magazine, **email your recipe, name, address, & phone number to: editor@homemademagazine.com**
> or mail to: HOMEMADE Magazine
> **333 Semoran Commerce Place**
> **Apopka, FL 32703**

Place this page in an envelope with your name and address and mail to:

Try-Foods International, Inc.
Attn: Wal-Mart "HOMEMADE" Magazine Fulfillment Dept.
333 Semoran Commerce Place
Apopka, FL USA 32703

(While supplies last. Allow 4 to 6 weeks for delivery.)